Reflections of the Game

LIVES IN BASEBALL

KEITH HINES - MEDICINE HAT BLUE JAYS

WILLOW CREEK PRESS

Minocqua, Wisconsin

© Willow Creek Press, Inc., 1998
Photographs © Ronald C. Modra

Published by Willow Creek Press
P.O. Box 147
Minocqua, Wisconsin 54548

For information on other Willow Creek Press titles, call 1-800-850-9453.

Cover and book design by LC Design Services.

Library of Congress Cataloging-in-Publication Data
Modra, Ronald C.
    Reflections of the game : the photographs of Ronald C. Modra / essay by
Pat Jordan ; foreword by Bob Costas.
      p. cm.
    ISBN 1-57223-180-7
    1. Baseball players—United States—Biography.   2. Baseball players—
United States—Biography—Pictorial works.   I. Jordan, Pat.   II. Title.
GV865.A1M62   1998
796.357'092'273—dc21   98-24520
                                             CIP

ISBN 1-57223-180-7

Printed in Canada

Reflections of the Game

LIVES IN BASEBALL

WILL CLARK

THE PHOTOGRAPHS OF
Ronald C. Modra

ESSAY BY PAT JORDAN   FOREWORD BY BOB COSTAS

JIM SLATON

WILLIE MAYS

ERNIE BANKS

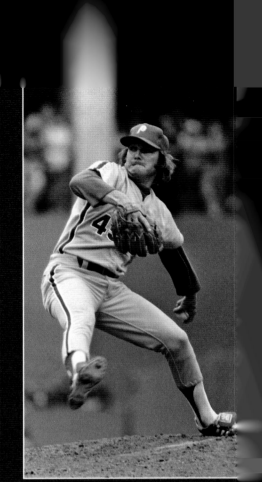

TUG MCGRAW

GEORGE SCOTT

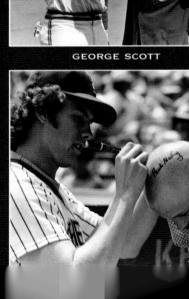

TOM BRUNANSKY

DAVE PARKER

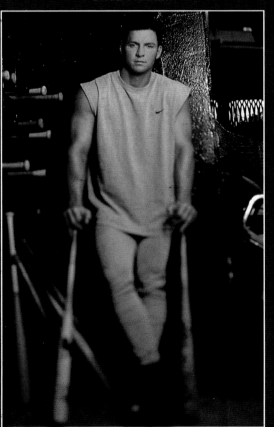

BRADY ANDERSON

MARK McGWIRE

JAY BELL

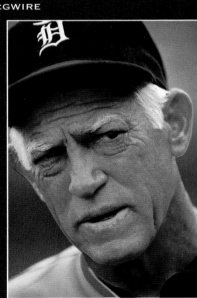

SPARKY ANDERSON

Acknowledgements

It took the efforts of a lot of people to make this book happen. Thanks to:

Herb Scharfman, who I met in Milwaukee in 1975, saw something he liked and brought me to New York City and to *Sports Illustrated*.

The *SI* Directors of Photography: John Dominus, Barbara Henckel, Neil Leifer, Joe Marshall, Karen Mullarkey, and Steve Fine.

The best assistants I could have, Phil Jache, Jim Keyser, Paul Schiraldi, Russ Davis, Jeff Salzer, Welsh Golightly, Jim Wenger, Lou Capozzola, Simon Dearden-Hose, Mike Dehoog, Dan Jenkins, and Scott Paulus.

Baseball editor Laurel Frankel, for 15 years of great editing and organizing. Thanks for putting up with me — and Laurel, get rid of some of the bad shoes.

John Iacono, the first *SI* shooter I ever worked with, for his long friendship.

Maureen Grise, the photo director on this book, whose research and input on this project made it work in spite of "Days" — who killed Kristen?

Pat Jordan, for a Herculean effort (it's always better to show and not tell), nuances, and showing me there was more — and life beyond *SI* — I hear you!

Ronnie Dunn and Kix Brooks, for giving me the opportunity to do something new and rediscover my enthusiasm for photography. Thanks for the confidence to bring me into the B&D family and for your friendship.

Tommy Burns, for always being willing to travel great distances. Not everyone brings their personal bartender with them.

Jodi and Doug Siewart, for showing me the real meaning of getting the job done.

Kelly Modra, daughter, pal and sometime assistant, I'm very proud of you! Do as I say, not as I do. Deanna — for those early years.

Sue Jordan, the biscuit queen — let's start dinner early so we can eat by midnight.

Mike Miller and Mel Levine in the *SI* stock room — Mel, I don't have that!

George Amores — *SI* Picture Collection, for his help in research.

Ray Foli, Ed Wagner and Bob Langer, and all my Chicago friends — thanks for letting me shoot at Wrigley in those early years.

Tom "Sky" Skibosh and Mario Ziino and all my friends at the Milwaukee Brewers.

All the PR Directors of major league teams who I bugged for additional access to the players.

Bud and Sue Selig who take the time to say hello at every World Series.

Phil Carter, Butch Jacobs, Mickey Palmer and all the fine folks at Topps Chewing Gum.

Phyllis Merhige, AL, save that #1!

Katy Feeney, NL VP.

Rusty Kennedy, thanks for running those remotes. Not bad for a Golden Girl!

John Walsh and Jim Drake at the real *Inside Sports*.

Rick Cerrone at the NY Yankees, before New York there was *Baseball Magazine*. Thanks, Rick, for the chance.

Everyone at Willow Creek Press — especially publisher Tom Petrie for believing in this project. Tom, I'm more of a walleye purist — no more sweet and sour!

Mom and Dad, I love you both — and see, I have been working all these years. Mom, go to work on those cookies.

A very special thanks to my longtime companion and now wife, MB Roberts. If not for her I might have given up on this book a long time ago. It's her encouragement that has kept me going. Love you.

And finally, especially, thanks to all the players and journalists who have participated in this book.

Dedication

To Herb Scharfman, who never saw the completion of this project. I hope he would be proud of it. I owe him so much. Herb was not only the *best* baseball shooter, but an incredibly kind man. All of us miss him.

— RCM

STEVE KEMP

LARRY WALKER

REGGIE JACKSON

LOU BROCK AND TED SIMMONS

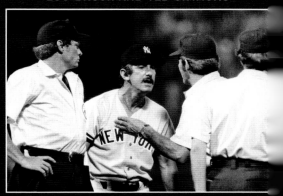

BILLY MARTIN

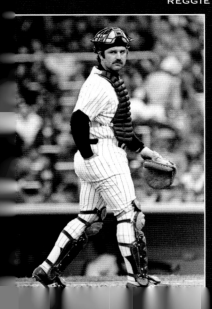

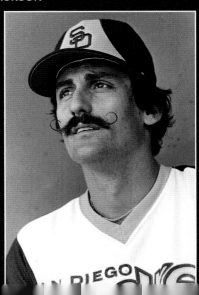

FOREWORD

Bob Costas

BY

There have probably been more words written and spoken about the beauty and appeal of baseball than all other sports combined. Hey, I've written and spoken some of those words myself. And yet, when it comes to conveying the hold the game can have on our imaginations, almost all of those words fall short of the power of a truly striking visual image. For 25 years now, Ron Modra has captured those images and moments with rare skill and understanding.

Baseball is a game of atmosphere and anticipation, punctuated by moments of brilliance and excitement. Like the game itself, Ron Modra's work has texture to it. From the ease of spring training to the tension of the World Series, from a kid in the stands to Ken Griffey, Jr. somehow climbing the fence to pull one out of the stands, Ron Modra captures it with a keen and appreciative eye.

The pages that follow are pure pleasure — the best work of a master craftsman and a guy who is one of us — a baseball fan.

— Bob Costas, *NBC Sports*

CHARLES JOHNSON - FLORIDA MARLINS, 1996

CAMDEN YARDS
BALTIMORE, MD 1992

Ronald C. Modra

BY

It's a balmy, clear October night in South Florida. The lights are on at Pro Player Stadium. A growing throng of people mill around on the brightly lit field. It's mostly clusters of reporters and guys in suits bumping into each other as they talk. Soon, Game 2 of the 1997 World Series will start. The Florida Marlins vs. The Cleveland Indians.

I am standing on a concrete slab just above the second level of seats. The slab is usually a TV camera platform, but tonight this six-foot space is my photo position, my own private balcony. I sit on a camera case and look down onto the field, wishing I had my baby Hibachi grill with me.

There is a slight breeze blowing. The energy in the stadium builds. I have been here for hours; I always get to games early. Tonight, I got here especially early because I had to lug the 1200, a huge camera lens I'll use to shoot from high above the outfield.

None of the four other *Sports Illustrated* photographers at the game wanted this outfield position. But I volunteered for it. From this position, getting a cover shot will be unlikely. But I don't care. I like it out here.

Every year more field credentials are given out for playoff and World Series games even though the space stays the same. You have to shoot with your elbows jammed into your ribcage. I'm getting old. It aggravates me now, as opposed to when I was starting my career, when I would have fought to be on the field. Out here, high above the players and other photographers, I have some space. I'm actually excited that I will have an angle no one else has. So I sit and do what I've spent most of my career doing: I wait.

A tall, burly guy with a handle-bar mustache calls to me through the locked gate behind our slab. He's wearing a uniform so I open the gate. He's a paramedic.

"Hey," he asks. "Could I stand out here just during the National Anthem?"

"Sure, why not," I say, pushing my camera case over to make some room.

"This is incredible!" he says. "I've got chills! I've never been to a World Series game before. Have you?"

"Yeah," I say.

"Which one? Last night?" he asks.

"Actually," I say, "I've been to all of them. Since 1980, anyway."

"Man!" he says.

We both turn our eyes to home plate as the teen pop group Hanson begins to sing "The Star Spangled Banner." (I know it's Hanson only because the paramedic told me.) He has his right hand over his heart. I put mine on my chest, too.

Hanson finishes. The crowd cheers. I look down at the field where the Marlins are jogging to their positions. Left-fielder Moises Alou, whom I have photographed many times in the U.S. and at his home in the Dominican Republic, turns to look into the crowd. He spots me and breaks into a big, warm smile. He gives me an exaggerated salute. I salute back. Then he winks and gives me the "thumbs-up." He puts his game face back on then turns to shag a ball.

OZZIE GUILLEN AND GLENN BRAGGS, 1986

JACK MORRIS AND DAN GLADDEN
WORLD SERIES: TWINS VS. BRAVES, 1991

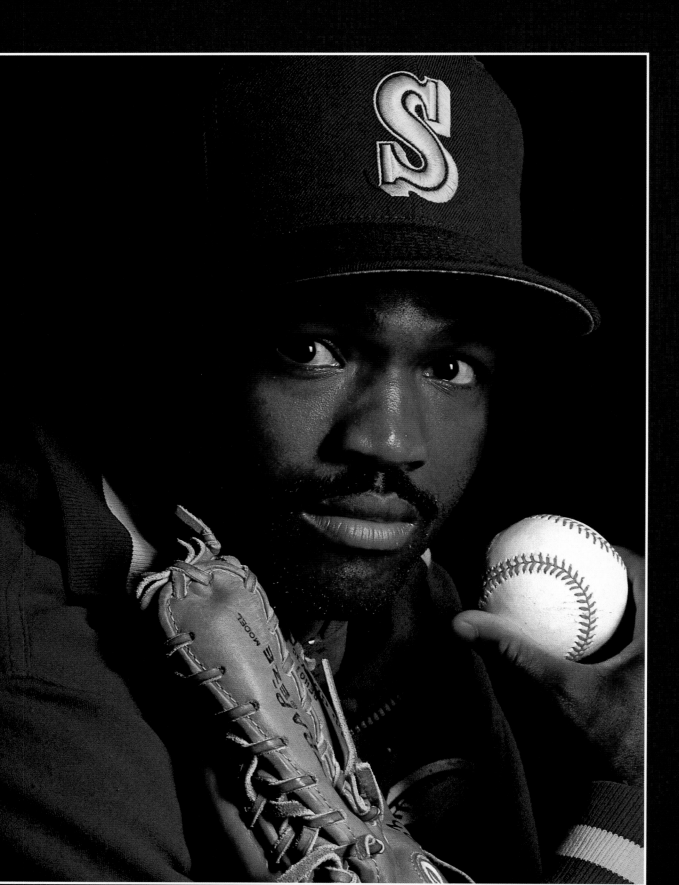

"I heard he's a great guy," the paramedic says.

"The best," I say.

Then the paramedic takes both my hands in his and says, "Thanks, man." He takes a big gulp of air then disappears through the gate.

For a moment, I feel really good. The feeling lasts through the next innings. Even David Justice waves and smiles at me when the Indians take the field. I laugh out loud, remembering my last trip to David's home in Atlanta. I was photographing him for a *Sports Illustrated* feature story. When I came for our appointment, he shut the door in my face, as well as the faces of my assistant and his agent, and left us standing on his terrace in 100-degree heat wondering if we should stay or go. This after a week of no-shows and calling me "the stalker" each time he encountered me at the ballpark.

I'm feeling so good tonight I wave back at David anyway.

My mind drifts, and I remember some of the World Series games I've worked. Yankees/Dodgers in 1981. Brewers/Cardinals in 1982. Braves/Twins in 1991. I remember how good I always felt. How different each one was.

Tonight, out here alone, I feel a great sense of fulfillment having spent almost my entire life around this game.

• • • • •

When I was eight years old, growing up in a tiny, Wisconsin town, I used to lay in bed at night listening to Milwaukee Braves games through the earpiece attached to my transistor radio. When the Braves played on the West Coast, the games came on late (10:00 PM). I would fight off sleep listening to broadcasters Blaine Walsh and Earl Gillespie.

"Holy cow! Home run!" Gillespie said when Hank Aaron, my favorite player, cracked another one. I'd hang on as long as I could, three innings at most. In the morning, I'd run down to ask my dad who won.

In 1957 and '58, when the World Series was played during the day, we got to watch the games at school. Even better than that, though, was going to games. My dad took me to County Stadium in Milwaukee a couple times a year. I was always excited to be there. Once we went early and I pressed against the fence trying to get Eddie Matthews' autograph. He wasn't signing that day. (I finally got his autograph 30 years later, when I found him on the barstool next to mine — but that's another story.)

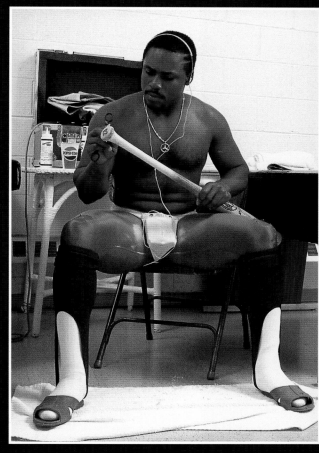

KEVIN MITCHELL - NEW YORK METS, 1986

LENNY DYKSTRA AND BOBBY BONILLA
THREE RIVERS STADIUM, PITTSBURGH, 1987

The last game I went to as a kid was Warren Spahn's 300th win on August 11, 1961. We sat in the cheap seats on the first-base side. I remember that because "Spahnny" was a leftie. It was great.

When I was in high school in the mid-60s, the Braves moved to Atlanta. There were no more games, so for fun, when I wasn't hunting or fishing, I worked with my dad at his printing company. That place was a sanctuary for me. In the mornings, I drove my mom to school. (She worked in my high school cafeteria.) I'd drop her off by the door. When she was out of sight, I'd drive to the plant and work all day, burning stencils or shooting color separations on the process camera. That was my first exposure to photography, besides playing around with the little Brownie camera that my grandmother gave me.

I collected baseball cards, hundreds of them. I had everyone from Aaron and Matthews to Willie Mays and Roger Maris.

When I went to Vietnam in 1967, my mother threw away my card collection. For years we've teased her about it, telling her I had Mickey Mantle's rookie card and could buy a house with it today. The truth is, I'm not sure I had the Mick.

When I returned from Vietnam, my father had sold his business. I got a job with another printer, intending to become a journeyman cameraman, the best-paying union job I thought I could get. I also began night-school photography classes. My first school assignment was a news photograph. That's all it took for me to know I wanted to do editorial photography instead of color separations.

Making pictures, even on the process camera, engaged me completely. I am a very hyper person but found myself calm, even patient, while shooting. But news photographs were always different and challenging. I could no longer imagine myself shooting the same stuff over and over on a process camera in a darkroom for the rest of my life. I wanted to be a news photographer so I could work outside. So no one day would be the same as another.

I then met the owner of the *Cedarburg News Graphic* who needed a weekend sports photographer. I hadn't thought about doing sports but it sounded great. I took the job. One year later, he offered me a full-time job (7 days a week) doing sports and news. I took it, even though by giving up my printing job I was cutting my income in half and losing my benefits.

For one of my news assignments I was sent to the county jail around midnight. A prisoner had died in his cell. I photographed the scene and then was asked to photograph the prisoner's autopsy. It was Halloween. I decided that night to begin concentrating on sports.

When a suburban weekly owned by the *Appleton Post Crescent* offered me a full-time sports job, I took it. I began getting credentials to shoot for the Milwaukee Bucks. John Steinmiller, who today

I worked on the Bucks' publication, *Pro Report*. A few years later, when *Pro Report* folded, my friend Sean Callahan and I attempted to resurrect it. I shot the whole thing. We thought it was a great paper. But no one bought it.

Soon after *Pro Report's* second untimely demise, I was offered the Brewers' team photographer job (Milwaukee had a team again). At that time, I had never shot a professional baseball game so I was nervous. But thrilled. I took the job even though it barely paid my expenses. To survive, I did as many freelance jobs, mainly basketball, as I could.

Like every sports-loving kid, I grew up reading *Sports Illustrated*. Being from Wisconsin, I of course was a fan of Green Bay Packer team photographer Vernon Biever, whose pictures appeared frequently in *Sports Illustrated*. When I started working as a photographer, I began studying the magazine. Every week I poured over the pictures by John Zimmerman, Jim Drake, Neil Leifer, Walter Iooss, Mark Kauffman, Johnny Iacono and Herb Sharfman.

Then in 1975, Herb Sharfman came to Milwaukee to photograph Hank Aaron. Since I was team photographer for the Brewers I got to show him around and we immediately became friends. He convinced me to send my "portfolio" (which was a Kodak box full of loose slides and black-and-white prints) to an editor at the magazine, Laurel Frankel.

Laurel showed them to the director of photography, John Dominus, saying, "We should take a look at this guy." Dominus was very positive, but nonetheless, his assistant, Don Delliquanti, sent me a letter which basically said, "Hey kid, your pictures are good but don't call us, we'll call you." I called anyway. Every week or two for several months until finally, probably because they were sick of hearing from me, I got an assignment to shoot a black-and-white picture of Rick Langston of the Oakland A's for a column.

After that I began doing small baseball assignments in Minneapolis, Kansas City, and Chicago. I was also freelancing for *Sport Magazine, Petersen's Baseball,* and Topps. But my goal was to work for *Sports Illustrated* full time.

After freelancing for *Sports Illustrated* for several months, I made a trip to New York City, where Herb introduced me to John Dominus. After that my assignments got a little meatier. I got my first cover — of the Detroit Lions' Billy Simms. I did football, basketball, tennis, and boxing. But still, baseball was my favorite. I liked the game better. Photographing baseball always reminded me of fishing. You wait and wait. Innings pass with nothing. Then when you least expect it, there's a big hit or a tangled play at the plate.

KEN GRIFFEY, JR. AND SR.
CINCINNATI, OHIO, 1989

Then, I was thrown the proverbial curve. My colleague Jim Drake was leaving his staff position at *SI* to become director of photography at *Inside Sports*. *Newsweek* was backing it at the time and everybody believed it was going to be a great magazine. (John Walsh, now of ESPN, was managing editor.) Jim offered me a contract. I felt I would get much better assignments at *Inside Sports* so I accepted. Then, much to my surprise, Dominus offered me an *SI* contract. It killed me, but I told him I had already committed to *Inside Sports.*

I worked there for one year. It was a great place to work. (Ironically, Pat Jordan, my good friend who wrote the essay for this book was also contributing to *Inside Sports* at the time, although we never met. We knew of each other, though. I heard a lot about him — everybody was talking about his controversial Steve Garvey story. We finally met in 1991 when I moved to Ft. Lauderdale.)

In 1981 *SI's* managing editor, Gil Rogin, called and offered me a contract. This time, I jumped on it. I never regretted it.

I covered different sports all over the place. I visited China, Russia, Australia, New Zealand, Japan, England, Germany, Sweden, France, Italy, Hungary, Czechoslovakia, Canada, Mexico, South America and all over the Caribbean, even to Cuba. I loved visiting these places, but the highlight of every year for me was the beginning of spring training.

I loved returning to the camps each February to see old friends. It has been fun for me growing up in the game along with players such as George Brett, Robin Yount and Paul Molitor, who were all rookies around the time that I was. Since I saw the same players over and over again every year, I always felt a responsibility toward them. I wanted them to like the pictures I shot. I tried to treat them with respect. I appreciate those players who treated me with respect in return. I am especially thankful to those who contributed "reflections" to this book.

Putting together this book has been incredibly gratifying. My life has been baseball. Doing this book made me feel proud of that. It was fun pouring over thousands of slides and reliving 25 years.

Finishing *Reflections of the Game* has made me feel at peace about sometime soon having to abandon that six-foot slab of concrete above the second level of stadium seats. *Sometime.*

THE END

RICK SUTCLIFFE
WRIGLEY FIELD, CHICAGO, 1984

Pat Jordan

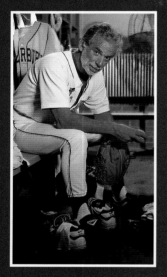

**WRITER PAT JORDAN
DRESSED FOR HIS
TRUE VOCATION.**

I was five years old when I began my love affair with baseball that has lasted these past fifty years. It was encouraged all along by my parents, second generation Italian-Americans. My mother loved the New York Yankees. Joe DiMaggio. Phil Rizzuto. Tony Crosetti. Tony Lazzari. Yogi Berra. Vic Raschi. And to a much lesser extent, Allie Reynolds, Hank Baurer, Gene Woodling, and Whitey Ford. Even today, at 90, my mother still has a photograph of Dave Righetti taped to the mirror in her kitchen.

My father, a professional gambler, loved the Yankees too. Only for him they were less a team he could point to with ethnic pride than a team he could confidently lay 9–to–5 on.

My aunt Josephine and uncle Ken were the only members of our family to own a television set in the late 1940s. So all the members of our family — my parents and I, uncle Ben and aunt Ada and uncle Pat and aunt Marie — would congregate there every Sunday afternoon in the summer to watch the Yankees play. It was always the Yankees because they were mostly Italians who were a credit to our ancestry. They had mastered the great American pastime of baseball as no other team ever had. They were a link to the country of our ancestry and the country that took us in as starving immigrants. DiMaggio, of course, was the greatest player in the game. The poor fisherman's son from the wharves of San Francisco who became a national hero in his adopted land. He not only mastered the American pastime, but also American ways. He played the game and moved through his life with style and grace and dignity that was a credit to Italian-Americans. He gave a lie to the stereotype of the loud, coarse Italians we had been burdened with for years. He was our strong, silent Gary Cooper. An Italian-American who had assimilated American Virtues without having lost his Italianness. He, alone, helped us forget Mussolini and the Mafia and even Frank Sinatra, who were black clouds hanging over Italian-Americans.

CONTINUED ON PAGE 31

**BRUCE BENEDICT - ATLANTA BRAVES
BUSCH STADIUM, ST. LOUIS, 1979**

STAN MUSIAL

LOU WHITAKER

The men sat in easy chairs in aunt Joe's living room and watched the Yankees play on my aunt's tall, mahogany Motorola TV set with a tiny, round, black-and-white screen. They smoked Chesterfields and drank White Label while the women hovered over pots of spaghetti sauce in the kitchen. They sipped scotch and smoked cigarettes, too, while they fantasized about the handsome Joe DiMaggio.

"Soooo handsome," my aunt Marie said, with a dreamy smile.

"He needs a good Italian wife," said aunt Joe, ever practical.

"If only your daughters were old enough," my mother said to aunt Joe.

My aunt Marie held up a huge sausage link she was about to drop into the sauce. She said something in Italian to her sisters. They laughed.

My mother held her hands about twelve inches apart and rolled her eyes heavenward.

"Mammamia!" said aunt Joe. "What a big bat!"

"Your poor daughters," my mother said.

"He'll probably marry some Irisher," said aunt Marie.

My mother and aunt Joe turned on her. "Never!" they said in unison. "Not Joe D. Never!"

In the living room the men were hunched forward in their chairs watching Yogi Berra at bat. Berra was squat, homely, taciturn, hard-working. The men loved him, but the women had little interest in him.

"That Yogi," said uncle Ben. "He's a tough one. A clutch batter."

"Not as good as Campanella," said uncle Ken. The two men began to argue over the relative merits of Yogi Berra and Roy Campanella of the Brooklyn Dodgers. Finally, my father intervened.

"What difference does it make?" he said. "They're both Italians." The men all nodded in agreement.

Finally uncle Pat said, "What about that time Campanella struck out? Berra would never have done that."

I was eight years old when I first began to play baseball seriously. Every summer morning I would pedal my bicycle to the baseball park near my house. My dog, Lady, a collie, would run alongside me. She followed me everywhere. She stood, panting beside me, in right field on the Little League diamond whenever I was lucky enough to be chosen by one of the older boys for those seemingly endless games of pick-up we played that summer. They always sent me to

CONTINUED ON PAGE 36

Hank Aaron

In early 1975, I was the Milwaukee Brewers' team photographer. Hank Aaron had just been traded to Milwaukee from the Atlanta Braves at his request. He wanted to finish his career where it began, in Milwaukee. The Home Run King was back. Aaron was the talk of the team and the town.

Later that year, the Brewers headed to spring training camp in Sun City, Arizona. One afternoon, I was loading equipment into my old, beat-up blue and white '69 van, having finished for the day. My van was the only vehicle in the parking lot. Everyone else had left the ballpark for the day. Or so I thought.

"Hey! You going back to the hotel?" someone shouted.

I turned around and saw Hank Aaron jogging toward me.

"Sure," I said, opening the passenger door for him.

I had photographed him twice, but this was the first time we were alone together. My heart pounded as I started up the van. As we drove, I wished someone I knew would pull up beside me and see who my passenger was.

I asked Aaron how he felt about being back. We chatted about the old Braves teams from the 50s. I was telling him about growing up in Milwaukee when he said, "Man, did you drive *this* all the way from Milwaukee?"

He was looking over his shoulder behind his seat, noticing the old mattress I slept on during the three-day drive from Wisconsin to Arizona.

"Yeah," I said sheepishly.

Aaron eyeballed the rusted interior, the ripped curtain behind the driver's seat, the burger wrappers on the floor, the broken radio.

Chuckling, he said, "I really think you should leave it here."

"HE WANTED TO FINISH HIS CAREER WHERE IT BEGAN, IN MILWAKUEE. THE HOME RUN KING WAS BACK."

RCM

Mike Schmidt

The fans in Philadelphia affected my play in a negative way. It was the nature of the Philly Beast. They grew up learning to boo players from their parents. It was my nature to rebel against that. Philadelphia was an ethnic town where people lived and died for their team. They expected players to have dirty uniforms. When they didn't see it, they got angry.

My personality created a clash with those fans. Being truthful with the press also got me in trouble. Whatever I said in the morning papers, I heard it from the fans that night. Yet they loved guys like Greg Luzinski, the Bull. He played hard and looked like one of them. I appeared aloof to the fans. Like the game came easy to me. When I failed, they said "He's not trying, because we know how easy it is for him."

They never saw me working behind the scenes with blisters on my hands.

In my day, the way to be was cool, like Joe DiMaggio. That's the way the great players carried themselves. It's the way I wanted to carry myself. Today players want to be showmen. They want to make a scene and bring as much attention to themselves as possible. That's the opposite of the great players I admired. If Joe D. had played in Philadelphia, he would have been scrutinized like me, too. The Philly fans like players like Len Dykstra who spit all over themselves and dive back into the dirt to first base when they could have just as easily stepped on the bag.

> ...DAY PLAYERS WANT TO BE SHOWMEN."
>
> MS

Dale Murphy

> "IT'S ALWAYS EASY TO PLAY FOR A WINNER, EVERYONE ON THE TEAM IS HAPPY."
>
> DM

I was traded to Philadelphia in 1990 after playing 15 years for the Braves. It was one of the more challenging moments of my career. I felt it was time to move on from the Braves. Then in 1991 the Braves went to the World Series. I had to question myself whether it had been wise to move on after trying to get to the World Series for all those years. But it was my decision. I had told the Braves if they wanted to trade me, go ahead. I was really struggling with the Braves at the age of 35. It was a tough decision for everyone, but I thought it was a good move. It was a tough blow to my ego.

When I retired a few years later, it wasn't like anyone missed me. I might have stayed with the Braves if I knew what changes they were going to make. It's always easy to play for a winner, everyone on the team is happy. They're all willing to not be concerned with personal statistics. You're all out for the same thing. The crowds are exciting. And other good players on your team make you play better.

right field, where, they assumed, I, an eight-year-old among twelve-year-olds, could do the least damage. I always batted ninth, and even then they tried to bat around me when I wasn't paying attention.

"Hey! It's my bats!" I would shout at the plate, facing the pitcher who looked so big to me then. My teammates shouted confusing instructions to me from the bench. "Hold the bat higher. Higher! Farther back! Spread your legs! Oh gee, not like *that*! Swing!" Invariably, I struck out on three pitches. My teammates grabbed their gloves in disgust and trotted out to the field.

"I told ya!" they hissed at me.

I ran to right field with tears in my eyes. I pounded my glove and assumed my outfielder's stance. Lady jumped and barked around me. I ignored her, lost in my shame. Lady grabbed the cuff of my jeans in her mouth and yanked. I tried to shake her off. I heard the

crack of the bat against the ball and looked up to see the ball sailing over my head. Lady ran after the ball. I ran after her. She scooped it up in her mouth and ran to the pond behind the right-field foul line. My teammates shouted behind me, "No! Stop her!" They came running too. But we were all too late. Lady waded out into the center of the pond, looked at us with the ball in her mouth, and then dropped it into the water.

On my way home from the park, I always stopped at the drugstore for a chocolate malt and to read copies of *Sport* magazine about my favorite players. Whitey Ford. Vic Raschi. Allie Reynolds. The pharmacist made Lady wait outside for me. She stared through the glass door looking pitiful while I sat at the counter on a round, swivel stool, spilling my milkshake over the magazines I never bought. The pharmacist just shook his head in despair, but said nothing.

One day at the park, I was standing in right field when I saw a car pull up in the gravel parking lot behind the third-base line. A man got out. He was tall and lean with sandy colored hair. The play on the field stopped. All eyes turned toward the man. He went to the back of his car, a station wagon, and opened the rear door. He pulled out a long canvas bag, hefted it onto his shoulders, and walked over to the third-base bench. All the boys but me ran wildly toward him. I stood, confused, in right field. The man upended the bag and its contents spilled out in the dust. Baseball bats. Balls. Catcher's shin guards. Chest protector. Plastic batting helmets with protective flaps, like earmuffs. One of the older boys began waving for me. He shouted, "Come on, stupid. It's the Little League coach."

I ran to him just as he was telling the boys he would call out each position and that they should raise their hands for the one they wanted to try out for. I was still panting from my long run from right field and my heart was pounding with excitement. I couldn't control my enthusiasm at the thought of being on my first real team. I shot up my hand at the first position he called out.

"Pitcher!" he said.

● ● ● ● ●

I loved being a part of that Little League team. The uniforms, the camaraderie, my teammates, even if, as an eight-year-old, I rarely played that first year. The games were played at twilight before a small crowd sitting on skeletal wooden slats for bleachers. The young mothers in Bermuda shorts chatted among themselves like magpies, stopping only to change their newest baby's diaper or glance down through the wooden slats to chastise their small sons

CONTINUED ON PAGE 42

Pudge Rodriguez

In July of '97, Pudge Rodriguez was the hottest catcher in baseball. He had just re-signed with his team, the Texas Rangers, after much speculation that he might be lured by a huge salary offer to another team. But he stayed. And that was news. So I traveled to Arlington, Texas to photograph him for an *SI* cover story.

I was to photograph Pudge at his house on July 3rd, which was also my 49th birthday. I was excited about this assignment, but I couldn't help but feel a little glum about spending my birthday and the fourth of July on the road.

My wife suggested I pretend it wasn't my birthday. I decided to try this approach as I pulled into Pudge's driveway. I went to work.

First, I set up a shot in front of a huge mirror in the upstairs bathroom where Pudge practices his stance. Then I waited. In the bathroom. Ten minutes. Fifteen minutes. I looked around. I noticed that Pudge was a Right Guard man. I wondered, does he really believe in this product or is it just another one of his endorsements? I looked in the mirror. Hmmm. A little gray. Forty-nine years old. Too old. Too old to be standing waiting for a twenty-something guy in his bathroom. I leaned toward the mirror to pluck an unusually long nosehair. I abruptly bolted upright when Pudge entered, bat in hand.

We finished then went outside. Pudge pointed toward the pool and told me he sometimes gets in waist-deep and practices swinging his bat.

"Great!" I said. "Let's do it."

"No," Pudge shook his head. "Not today."

I took off my cap to wipe the dripping sweat off my forehead.

"Why not?" I asked.

The hottest catcher in baseball answered, "It's too cold."

The next day, the fourth of July, we were supposed to do a family shot but his son was at a picnic and didn't return in time. Now there was pressure to come up with a cover shot. On my way to the ballpark before that night's game, I tried to think of an idea. I wanted something that popped. Something that looked like game action.

Pudge is an emotional player. He pumps his fist in the air when he throws out a runner at second. I wanted something like that and knowing I might not get it during the game, I brought Pudge to the bullpen before batting practice and stood him against the green wall. I said, "O.K., do your thing. Scream! Shout! Throw somebody out!"

He gave a great performance, which became one of my favorite covers. I knew we had it so I relaxed during the game. Afterward, I even stayed to watch the fireworks.

A REFLECTION BY

Paul Molitor

My most vivid memory in baseball is the time I met Ted Williams at a dinner in '94. I had always wanted to meet him. I was seated at a head table with Joe DiMaggio, Sandy Kofax and Ted. Ted's son came up to me and said, "Dad's excited to meet you."

I said, *"What?"*

When I met Ted, he jumped to his feet so quickly it was overwhelming. Before I could ask him anything, he started telling me about my batting stance, my thought process, and how I reminded him of Joe DiMaggio. Ted was able to stay in a quiet approach until the ball was in his zone. Ted had the ability to break hitting down to things most normal people can't understand. It was something I'll never forget, being complimented by one of the all-time great hitters in baseball.

PAUL MOLITOR

fooling around under the stands.

The fathers, in loosened ties and rolled-up shirt sleeves, came directly from work. They stood around behind the home-plate screen, like Indian scouts surveying the horizon. They shaded their eyes with the flat of their hands as they tried to follow the unfolding action on the field, under the harsh orange light of the sun setting behind a line of trees beyond right field.

A college boy sat at a folding card table behind the home-plate screen. He kept the official scorecard and worked the record player that played only the National Anthem to begin games, and, between innings, choruses of "They Call the Wind Maria," by Frankie Lane. He was surrounded by boys and girls my age on bicycles. The boys leaned against the home-plate screen, gripping it with their fingers, heedless of the umpire's warning that a foul tip could smash their fingers. The umpires were gnarled, unshaven, ex-ballplayers of local repute who had once starred in the Senior City League for the White Eagles A.C. or the Rosebuds or the Savoy A.C. Now, in their fifties, they still liked to keep their hand in the game. They parked their cars in the right-field lot and waited, sipping coffee, until game time before beginning their long, heavy-bellied, pigeon-toed walk to home plate. Some of them worked as stone masons. Their skin was coated with a fine white powder. Some were carpenters with gnarled hands criss-crossed with cuts and purple bruises. When they reached home plate they acknowledged, with a nod, the respectful greetings of those fathers who remembered them from their playing days.

Before the game was more than a few innings old, a dozen girls, high-school cheerleaders, would assemble underneath the maple tree beyond the left-field fence. They formed a chorus line, and led by their blonde captain in jeans rolled up to her knees, they began practicing their cheers for the upcoming football season. I never noticed them when I was eight and nine, but when I turned eleven, and had become a Little League star pitcher, they suddenly seemed so exotic to me, like colorful, tropical birds. They kicked their tanned legs high, in unison, and their voices rang out with incongruous football cheers amid the sounds of the Little League game in progress.

When I was ten, I became my team's star pitcher. It separated me for the first time from my peers. It was my first distinction in life; the first thing I could do well others my age couldn't. People came from surrounding towns to see me pitch. They pointed me out,

CONTINUED ON PAGE 46

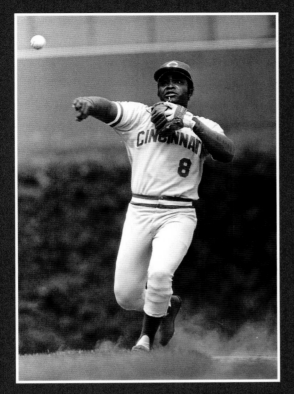

JOE MORGAN

SIXTO LISCANO

BERT CAMPANARIS
MILWAUKEE COUNTY STADIUM

CHAN HO PARK
VERO BEACH, FLORIDA, 1994

called out my name, applauded my strikeouts. Old men of distant local repute followed my pitching with interest. I saw them nod to one another after I struck out a batter. A sign. But of what? Parents looked at me with big eyes and introduced me to their younger sons, and daughters, as if I was someone special. Sometimes their daughters were older, thirteen and fourteen, and had no interest in me — a boy of ten. But I was beginning to have an interest in them. When I turned eleven, then twelve, a big boy for my age, those girls began to reciprocate my interest. I could see them behind the home-plate screen, hanging back a bit, but watching me through narrowed eyes, wondering when I would catch up to them. It excited me. All the attention. The old men nodding to me as I passed in my uniform after another no-hitter. The parents smiling at me. Their daughters, staring. They confused me. I averted my eyes and blushed at their brazen, appraising smiles.

I lost myself in the order and discipline of the game, and my small stardom. It was an escape from my parents' house where my father's gambling losses, all our losses, were beginning to have a deleterious affect on our family. When my parents had harsh words over my father's gambling, I left the house to play baseball. Ironically, my baseball seemed briefly to bring my parents closer together. They united around my pitching. My father bought me a $50 Herb Score model glove and kangaroo-skin baseball spikes. My mother never made me do chores on days I was to pitch. She made me a special dinner of eggs and sweet peppers fried in olive oil, with pizza *frite* (fried dough) sprinkled with powdered sugar for dessert. After supper, I rode my bicycle to the park in my uniform. Lady no longer went with me. She had to be locked up in the cellar because at the park during my games she would run onto the field to the pitcher's mound to be with me. She didn't understand that these games were now organized, were now *serious,* not like the pick-up games when I was eight. The fans would laugh at her, and me, as I dragged her off the field in embarrassment. On days I was to pitch, I'd drag Lady, whimpering, to the cellar and leave her there. Soon, whenever she saw me in my uniform, she would put her head down and slink down to the cellar of her own accord, her tail between her legs. Now she would not even follow me to the park when I didn't have an organized game no matter how hard I tried to coax her out of the cellar. I missed her at the park on those days.

CONTINUED ON PAGE 53

TONY GWYNN - SAN DIEGO PADRES, 1993

Barry Bonds

In 1994, Barry Bonds, the San Francisco Giants slugger and baseball's highest-paid man, was the subject of an *SI* cover story. The editors wanted a portrait that said "San Francisco." The Golden Gate Bridge had been done so my assistant and I headed to the cable car barn downtown. We arranged for the #25 car (Bonds' number) to be taken off the street and got permission to use it in a portrait with Bonds at the barn on his upcoming day off. The city would charge us $200 a day. We confirmed the shoot with the Giants' PR staff.

My assistant and I worked for several hours setting up the next morning. An *SI* editor talked to Bonds directly and offered to send a car to take him to the shoot. He said, no thanks. He knew where the car barn was. Our appointment was at noon. By 1:00, I was worried that he was lost so I stood on the street corner looking for him — till about 3:00. At 3:30 we struck the set.

The next morning, we set up again. Bonds said he would meet us at noon. At 1:00, Bob Rose, the Giant's Public Relations Director, called him on his car phone. He said he was on the way. We waited till 3:00. At 3:30 we struck the set.

We set up a third morning. A third time, no Bonds. At the game that night, I asked him if he was still interested in doing a portrait. He said yes. The Giants were leaving to play a series in New York. I returned to San Francisco when the team did and again obtained access to the cable car and created the set.

Bonds again was a no-show. When I ran into him in the clubhouse that night he said, "you'll just have to live with it, dude," and walked away. *Sports Illustrated,* under deadline pressure, put an action picture on the cover.

The cover story, "I'm Barry Bonds and You're Not," described the several weeks the writer spent being stood up by Bonds, who was evidently furious with the piece. One thing some players never learn: If you blow-off a photographer, you're really only hurting yourself because his job is to make you look good. The reason he is there is all about you. But blow-off a writer, and he or she will probably write about it.

"IF YOU BLOW-OFF A PHOTOGRAPHER, YOU'RE REALLY ONLY HURTING YOURSELF BECAUSE HIS JOB IS TO MAKE YOU LOOK GOOD."

RCM

"I remember whe[n] a child and reading t[he] ry books, I though[t] great things would be fun. It's been the o[...] This hasn't been fun a[...]

The media — pa[rticular]ly the white media ruined everything. [...] crucified me. They've me names. They've stones. They've tried tray me as some horri[ble] son, a monster, like animal.

Do you think if I s[...] a separate hotel fr[om the] team like Cal Ripken [...] would be said? I w[ould] crushed in the media, I have been my entire [...]

Jesus spoke the [...] the time, but not ev[eryone] liked him, either.

I'll disappear, go Hall of Fame cereme[...] years later, and th[...] won't ever see me ag[ain]"

BARRY

BARRY BONDS

Goose Gossage

I'm the only player in the major leagues to go through all four work stoppages from 1972 to 1994. The last one hurt me a lot. I was pitching well at Seattle and then the strike came, and after the strike was over I couldn't get a job anymore. Playing this game is so fragile anyway. I mean, one pitch and you're out of the game. Those strikes take the innocence, beauty, fun and love out of the game.

Money ruins a lot of things. In 1972, my first year, I would have played for nothing. Hey, I was putting on a big league uniform. It's a shame money reared its ugly head the way it does. Although I do believe the players deserve the money they're making. Years ago, players were under contract for life and they were screwed.

The Marlins winning the World Series in 1997 and then breaking up their team was the most bizarre thing I ever saw. I was broken-hearted. Years from now, people won't even remember who was on that team. I hope this is a once-in-a-blue-moon scenario. If it's a trend, baseball is in big trouble. The fans are taken for granted on both sides — by the owners and players.

The owners don't do a very good job putting together their teams. We as a union don't conduct ourselves as we should with the public. Some players' attitude is "screw the public." But we should try to get the fans back on our side. But I guess to expect baseball to be pure when the whole world has changed is unfair. But it's still a great game.

'IN 1972, MY FIRST YEAR, I WOULD HAVE PLAYED FOR NOTHING.'

GG

Nolan Ryan

" . . . ONE OF
MY FAVORITE
MOMENTS WAS
PLAYING WITH
MY SON."

NR

The first thing that comes to mind when I think of memorable moments is when Morgana came running onto the field at the Astrodome and kissed me! But seriously, I would have to say one of my favorite moments was playing against my son. When he was at the University of Texas, the Texas Rangers played an exhibition game against the UT baseball team. I pitched for the Rangers and Reid was pitching for them. There were so many emotions going on in that game for me. I was trying to concentrate on my pitches and the game, but I was also a dad with pride and concern for my son. I will always have fond memories of that experience.

MINOR-LEAGUE PLAYER
MEDICINE HAT, ALBERTA, CANADA, 1990

My parents went to all my games. They sat high in the skeletal wooden bleachers along the third-base line. A couple. Respectable now. My father not a gambler, now, but *my* father, his new-found distinction. Other parents pointed them out, acknowledged them with respectful hellos. Doctors, lawyers, judges. They all complimented my parents on my pitching. "A fine boy," they'd say, "You should be proud." It was as if, to those parents, my talent on the mound implied some qualities of inner character that other boys my age, who could not throw a baseball as fast as I could, somehow lacked.

My mother beamed at these compliments, at this respectability my pitching brought her. She cheered my every pitch. When I got two strikes on a batter I would hear her shrill voice call out, "Strike him out, Patty!" From the mound, I looked at them, winked, turned back to the batter and struck him out. I looked back and saw my mother clapping her hands with glee, while my father leaped down behind the stands and half walked, half ran toward the pay telephone near the tennis courts to call his bookie.

• • • • •

He stood on the pitcher's mound with a baseball in his hand — a tall, gangling boy of twelve in a Little League uniform that was so small on him, the pants barely reaching his knees, that he resembled a stick figure. I remember he had a long face and pale skin and a frightened look in his wide, unblinking eyes that looked like the eyes of an animal trapped in a hunter's sight.

He didn't look like a pitcher, not even a Little League pitcher. He had to pause a second before each pitch to remind himself how to put his foot on the rubber, and then how to pump, and kick, and lunge, and follow through so that he was squared to the batter now only a few feet away. And as he went through his motion, step by awkward step, he watched himself to make sure he got it right. He watched himself with such simple concentration, his brow knitting, that he seemed to forget entirely about the batter.

He had been recruited to pitch by his coach, the produce manager at a local supermarket, because he was so much taller than the other boys his age. His coach felt his size alone would frighten batters in a way his talent, or rather, lack of talent, would not. But he frightened no one. On this clear summer day, in full view of his

CONTINUED ON PAGE 56

FERGUSON JENKINS
GUTHRIE, TEXAS, 1991

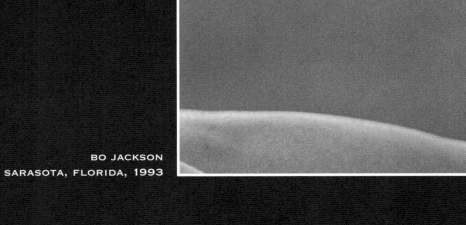

BO JACKSON
SARASOTA, FLORIDA, 1993

parents, the fans, other boys and girls his age, and myself, seated in the stands along the third-base line, he could not retire even the tiniest of batters. The fans laughed at him at first. "Imagine! A boy his size!" And then they began to feel sorry for him. "He's trying so hard," said a mother seated beside me.

With each succeeding base hit, the pitcher took more and more time between pitches, until he was almost immobile on the mound, unable to deliver another pitch. He looked toward the dugout for his coach with pleading eyes, but his coach was bent over, his hands cupped around a match, lighting a cigarette. The pitcher's shoulders sagged as he forced himself to begin his mechanical delivery once again. The batter hit a ground ball toward the mound. The pitcher followed it with his eyes, but he could not make himself reach down for it. The ball passed close to his right foot and continued on into center field. The pitcher remained frozen in his follow-through for a split-second as an idea trudged across his brow, and then he fell to the ground, clutching his left foot as he writhed in the dirt. His coach and teammates rushed toward him as the umpire called, "Time!" They hovered over him for a few minutes — his coach down on one knee, massaging his pitcher's foot — and then he struggled to his feet. He draped his arms over the shoulders of two smaller teammates — his arms like an eagle's wings over his chicks — and hobbled off the mound to applause from sympathetic fans.

That applause seemed to me then, as it does now, so false. It stemmed not only from the fans' sense of relief that the pitcher was not seriously hurt but also from their sense of relief that they would no longer have to watch his humiliation. The fans' sympathetic applause began to build as he crossed the third-base line. Only I was not so sympathetic. I yelled out, loud enough for everyone to hear, "That's one way of gettin' off the mound!" The fans booed and hissed at me. Somebody shoved me in the back. "You should be ashamed!" But I wasn't. Even as my face reddened under the fans' abuse, I knew I was right. He was a quitter. He didn't take it seriously. Like I did. At eleven. Already a Little League star. My name in headlines every week in the local newspaper. More strikeouts. Another one-hitter. Sports was a serious business for me even then, and I did not harbor much sympathy for anyone who did not take it as seriously as I did. I ran wind sprints to stay in shape. Imagine! At eleven!

It became obvious one summer day when I was eleven that my

talent was something special. At that time, my brother, George, fourteen years older than I, devoted his free time from his law practice to coaching me. He used to stop by our parents' house at lunch time to have a catch with me on the sidewalk in front of our house. Our parents sat on the front porch and watched. They applauded my pitches. I began my wind up and threw a fastball that cracked in my brother's catcher's mitt. He yanked out his hand and shook it fiercely to shake off the hot pain. And my parents applauded. My brother, tall, gangling, wearing a white button-down-collar shirt, the sleeves rolled up past his elbows, would grimace in both mock and very real pain as he shook his burning hand. How I responded to that gesture!

One day when George couldn't "work with me," as he used to call it, I badgered my father to catch me. My father, a lefty, had never been much of an athlete. He had been an orphan, and in his teens he turned to gambling for his satisfactions and his livelihood. He was not as passionately devoted to my pitching as George and I were. Even then, we thought of it less as a sport than as my career.

My father was in his early forties then, and, although he'd ceased to gamble full time, he was still a betting man. Occasionally he would deal cards at late-night poker games in the Venice A.C. He was an excellent dealer, and was paid well. It was in the hands, he said. His fingers were small and plump, like the sausages my mother threw in the spaghetti sauce, she said.

My father began to catch me with reluctance. He had to wear the catcher's mitt — meant for one's left hand — on his right hand. His little finger fit into the glove's fat thumb, which stuck out ridiculously. He grumbled as I threw. His mind was on the card game at which he would deal that night at the Venice A.C. "Fellow athletes," my mother used to say, and we'd all laugh.

Suddenly, to impress my father, I cut loose with a fastball. Startled, he caught it on the middle finger of his left hand, the one without the glove. The finger split open and blood spurted everywhere. He looked at his finger in disbelief, then ran bellowing into the house. When I finally got up the courage to go in, too, I saw him sitting at the kitchen table, his hand wrapped in a blood-soaked handkerchief. He was trying to deal a poker hand to my mother. She warned me with a glance to silence. The cards slipped in his bleeding hand. They began to slide down his wrist. He tried to pin them to his side with his elbow. They scattered across the floor. He glared at them, and began to curse. He snatched them up with his good hand and tried to deal again.

Years later we would all laugh at that scene — my mother and

CONTINUED ON PAGE 62

Pete Rose

In 1986, when Pete Rose was with the Phillies, I was assigned to photograph him doing his famous head-long dive. We couldn't wait around hoping he might do it during a game so he agreed to do it in a set-up situation.

SI initially sent another photographer to do the shot. Rose did a series of slides for the guy, but the pictures didn't turn out. *SI* sent me to do a re-shoot.

"Why didn't they send you the first time?" Rose asked me when I met up with him at the Phillies' spring training camp in Clearwater, Florida. I asked him when we could set up the shot again. He said, "I'm committed for something tomorrow, but we can do it Thursday at 4:00. I'll meet you when we get back from the game."

On Thursday, I set up early and started what I expected to be my usual waiting game. At exactly 4:00, the Phillies' bus pulled into the parking lot. Out came Rose, dressed and ready, waving at me.

"I'm only gonna do it eight times," he said.

I laughed. Most guys will do something, especially something where they could get hurt, only once, maybe twice, if at all.

Rose looked at me, and I nodded. He took off running and dove into third. He brushed himself off. "Again?" he said. I gave him thumbs-up. He did it again. And again.

"Pete, we've definitely got it."

"You sure? I'll do it again."

"No. We've definitely got it."

A few years later, when Rose was the manager/player for Cincinnati, I went to photograph him for an *SI* cover. He told me to meet him in his office at 11:00. I got there at 10:30. He was sitting at his desk waiting for me. He ushered me in immediately when he saw me and we went right to work. I photographed him in his office, in the dugout, on the field.

"You got everything you need?" he asked before heading to a meeting. I did. And then some.

"HE WAS
ENTHUSIASTIC,
LIKE A KID."

RCM

After Rose retired and had opened the Pete Rose Ballpark Cafe near his home in Boca Raton, Florida, I went to photograph him for a feature. First, I met him at the restaurant where he was doing a radio show. He told me he would sign autographs after the show for 15 minutes then meet me out front for a picture. He met me exactly 15 minutes after the show.

The next day I was to meet him at his house at 10:00. I arrived ten minutes early. Rose opened the door and showed us in. He offered my assistant and me something to drink. Then he gave us several ideas for pictures. "How 'bout the go-carts?" He was enthusiastic, like a kid.

Say what you want about Pete Rose. I'd work with him any day.

Kirby Puckett

It's harder to be a good guy than a bad guy in baseball — which is why there aren't that many good guys. I think the bad guys are not bad by nature, they're just misinformed.

I love baseball because I knew what it took for me to get here. Every day I had to walk on eggshells as a role model. I never thought of myself as a role model, but other people did. So that put pressure on me. If I did something wrong, there'd be a black cloud over my head for just that one blemish. Some guys use their anger as fuel to play the game. I never wanted to be angry, because we all are judged for the things we do.

I only worry about what I can control. I don't worry about getting into the Hall of Fame. I'm still a good human being. A lot of guys can't say that. They don't know what to do when the game is gone for them. I wear a suit and tie every day as a national spokesman for glaucoma and I'm loving it. Now I get to be a chauffeur for my kids. When I left the game I didn't skip a beat. It was my time. God works in mysterious ways. I knew I could have gotten 3,000 hits, but that's over now. My numbers speak for themselves. In my time, I was one of the best.

> "I LOVE BASEBALL BECAUSE I KNEW WHAT IT TOOK FOR ME TO GET HERE."
>
> KP

A   R E F L E C T I O N   B Y

Dwight Gooden

I'm a different pitcher today. As a kid, I just threw my fastball to batters when I got behind in the count. Today, I change speeds more. I'm a student of the game. I don't throw as hard consistently as I did when I was 20. But I haven't been in a mental zone the last few years. It's been tough ever since I spent a year out of the game in 1995.

I've made mistakes in my career. I pitched when I was hurt which led to surgery in '91. I had to learn not to trust everyone who approaches you as a friend. I was too trusting. I said yes too easily. I had to learn to speak my mind and not say yes to everyone.

As a kid I dreamed of being in the big leagues and having a nice career. But I never thought of awards until after the '85 season when I won the Cy Young Award. I'll never forget, after that I had a talk with my father. I told him I was going to win 20 games every year. But I didn't. Still, I couldn't be happier.

The record I'm most proud of was my 300 strikeouts in one minor league season when I was at Lynchburg, Virginia, in the Carolina League. I needed 14 strikeouts in the last seven innings of my final game and I got them. That record still holds up. I feel good when some young guys tell me they'd want a shot at the record.

me terrified, my father dealing, the cards spilling, curses and bloodstained kings. It became one of those anecdotes for which families invent a significance which, at the time, eluded them, but in retrospect grows to mythical proportions. The point became, *my speed!* I threw *that* hard! Hard enough, at eleven, to break a grown man's finger. It seems even then we were attuned to such small evidences of my destiny. I had a gift. We all shared in this gift. My father bought me the best gloves, my mother pampered me on days I would pitch, my brother "worked with me" on his lunch hour, and even my uncle Ben pitched in when I was twelve and in my last year of Little League. He became my team's coach.

• • • • •

My uncle Ben was a squarish-built man with dark skin and a hooked nose. His wiry gray hair was parted to one side in a Princeton cut. He dressed like a preppy — navy blazer, Gant shirt, gray flannel slacks — but always with a distinctive touch all his own. Suede wheat-colored loafers. He was a courtly man, with his own elegant style, like Cary Grant, who seemed boyish beyond his years. Maybe that was because he and aunt Ada could never have children of their own.

My uncle lived down the street from us in the suburbs. Every morning I'd walk to his house for breakfast. Always the same breakfast. One poached egg, a glass of orange juice, and perfectly tanned and buttered toast. A meager breakfast for a child, but my uncle made it seem a feast for a King. He made a great production of squeezing oranges by hand, timing our eggs, and buttering the toast with warm butter so it wouldn't dig up the bread the way cold butter would.

While we ate, uncle Ben read the major league box scores to me from the newspaper. He always began with the Yankees. Then, after I helped him wash the dishes, we went outside in his driveway to pitch. He got down stiffly into his catcher's crouch, pinching the knees of his elegantly pressed slacks so they would not wrinkle, and laying a piece of white cloth on the pavement as the plate. We made believe I was pitching to the Yankees. After each pitch, he would bounce out of his crouch like a boy and fire the ball back to me. "Atta boy, Patty! You got him!"

Like many childless adults, he didn't have to feign having fun with a child. He really did! He was fascinated with children, especially boys, all of whom reminded him of the son he never had.

Uncle Ben called balls and strikes as I worked my way down the Yankees' batting order. When I got to Joe D., I could feel myself tighten with fear at the mighty slugger whom I could see as a faint shadow there beside my uncle. Joe D. with his long nose and thick lips stood there, eyeing me, waiting for my best pitch. I tried to throw too hard and got behind in the count to Joltin' Joe, the Yankee Clipper. My face flushed with panic, even then, as if Joe D. was really there. Then my uncle, who was usually so hard on me, gave me a break on a pitch even I could see was off the plate. "Strike three!" He said, and fired the ball back to me. "You struck out the Clipper. Thata boy."

I always pitched a perfect game against the Yankees with uncle Ben. They could never hit me.

My uncle Ben was never comfortable around adults, with all their neuroses and duplicities, for in many ways he was as innocent

CONTINUED ON PAGE 66

DAVE WINFIELD
TORONTO SKYDOME,
1992

as a child. Maybe that's why he jumped at the chance to become my team's Little League coach when I was twelve. The job always came up every two years or so, since most of the coaches were fathers of one of the players. They coached until their son left Little League and then so did they. Even though uncle Ben had no children of his own, it was assumed he'd coach only until I left Little League and then he'd quit, too. But he never did. He was still the Little League coach twenty years after I'd left the team and was married with children of my own.

As my coach, my uncle was hard on me, harder than he was on the other players, all of whom he treated, not like children, but like small adults. We both knew his "hardness" was a ruse to hide his obvious affection for me. He called me "Jordan," not "Patty," and at practices he always made me carry the heavy canvas bag from his car to the field.

When he pitched batting practice he always made me bat last, even though I was leading the team in home runs, in addition to being its star pitcher. He wore chino slacks and a crewneck, shetland sweater as he threw, stiffly, like a man who'd come to baseball late in life. When I batted, he grunted a little harder on his fastball and always tried to fool me with his curve by not telling me it was coming as he did for the other players. It wasn't really much of a curve, just a little, lopsided spin and a last-second wrinkle. I made a point of bailing out of the batter's box on his curve just to make him feel good. He'd growl at me, "Come on, Jordan! Hang in there like a man!"

No matter how hard on me my uncle tried to be, he could never hide his pleasure in me when I pitched. I would be on the mound in the final inning of a game we were winning 1–0, and I would see him pacing back and forth in the dugout, yelling encouragement. "Come on, Patty! You can do it!" I wasn't "Jordan" *now*. When I struck out the last batter, my uncle would leap out of the dugout and run toward me. He was always the first to shake my hand, and then, catching himself, he shook the hands of every other player.

Despite my uncle's superficial sternness with me, and the others, he was not really a stern man. However, he could not abide "silliness" in his ballplayers. He called them "men" and ran herd on us to always act like "men." I remember one time, in particular. It was before a game I was scheduled to pitch. I was fooling around, showing off

CONTINUED ON PAGE 73

CARL YASTRZEMSKI

VIDA BLUE

JIM GANTNER
MILWAUKEE COUNTY STADIUM

George Brett

The first time I really got to know George Brett was right after his rookie year. Kansas City was playing Milwaukee and his former teammate, Jamie Quirk, new to the Brewers, introduced me to him. He and Quirk were good friends and Brett asked me if I would snap their picture together.

They posed with their arms around each other, but stood far apart, as if someone should be in the middle.

"Guys — stand closer together," I said. "You look ridiculous."

Then Brett explained that they meant to pose that way. The picture was for their former teammate who had been traded.

"This is for our friend," Quirk said. "We're gonna send it to him."

I gave Brett a print of the shot the next day so he could send it to their friend. He was appreciative, friendly and down-to-earth.

He remained that way over the years. We worked together many times as he became a bigger and bigger star. To me, he'll always be the young, fun-loving guy with his arm around an imaginary friend.

"TO ME,
HE'LL ALWAYS
BE THE YOUNG,
FUN-LOVING
GUY WITH
HIS ARM
AROUND AN
IMAGINARY
FRIEND."

RCM

MOISES ALOU'S GRANDMOTHER

A REFLECTION BY

Moises Alou

I never felt any pressure to follow the family into baseball. Actually, I never liked baseball that much when I was a kid. I liked basketball better. I got into baseball by accident. After I graduated high school I wanted to go to college in the states. But the only way I could go to college was to get a baseball scholarship. I got a baseball scholarship to a junior college in California. It took me six months of struggling with baseball before I improved. After all, I hadn't ever played organized baseball before.

MOISES ALOU AND HIS FATHER, FELIPE

CARLTON FISK AND TOM SEAVER
COMISKEY PARK, CHICAGO, 1985

really, behind the dugout for the benefit of some twelve-year-old girls whose mutual interest we'd both aroused. I put my cap on backward, and my spikes were unlaced in a sloppy manner to elicit laughter from those girls. My uncle heard the commotion and looked over the dugout roof. He snapped at me, "Fix your hat and spikes, Jordan! Look like a ballplayer!"

I sulked for the entire game. I felt humiliated. After the game, my uncle drove me home. I sat in glum silence beside him in my uniform. He tried to explain to me what I'd done wrong.

"It's important how your look, Patty." he said. "Those little details, like wearing your uniform just so, add up. They all count. If you do the little things right, then when the big things come along you'll know how to handle them. You'll be prepared. Disciplined. That's why it's important to pay attention to the little details. Sometimes the little details are all you'll ever have in life. You can learn to take satisfaction in them. It makes everything else worthwhile."

As a child of twelve, I only vaguely understood what he meant. He was talking about pride in yourself. Now, I understand, he was talking about something deeper, too. His own life. All those little details he mastered, that squeezed orange juice, that perfect toast, because there was no big thing in his life — a son — to look forward to.

People came from all over the state to see me pitch that year, 1953. Newspaper reporters interviewed my uncle. He discoursed on baseball and boys, and how to raise them, of all ironies, and also on the talents of his star pitcher, Jordan. He became sort of an acknowledged expert on the turning of young boys into little men. Reporters wrote about him as the Casey Steingel of Little League baseball, and, in truth, he was more than a little eccentric like Casey. But unlike Casey, he didn't know enough about baseball to really manage our team, so he kept things simple and orderly, his secret to success. We won every game that year by wide margins, 16–0, etc., etc. He knew the limits of his boys and he never pushed them beyond their limits. The other managers over-extended their players by concocting elaborate pick-off plays at second base that always backfired and humiliated those boys in front of laughing fans and their own parents. Those managers managed, not for the boys, but for themselves. To show the fans how much *they* knew. My uncle always managed in a way that kept the attention on us, not him. He knew

CONTINUED ON PAGE 76

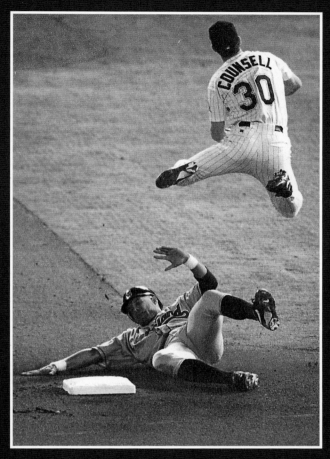

DAVID JUSTICE AND CRAIG COUNSELL
WORLD SERIES, PRO PLAYER STADIUM, 1997

OREL HERSHEISER
VERO BEACH, FLORIDA, 1993

he didn't really know much about baseball, so he just drilled us long and hard in the fundamentals and then let us play the game. He ran practices by his stop watch. BP–6:15 p.m. to 7:05 p.m. Infield–7:05 p.m. to 7:25 p.m.

Before our games, he hit fungoes to us during infield practice, firmly, but not with all his might. The other managers showed off by blasting the ball past their poor, befuddled infielders, and then, in embarrassment, had to let up on the next one, hitting a little dribbler that barely reached them and humiliated them even more. Uncle Ben made us look good by extending us precisely to, but never beyond, our limits. And each game those limits progressed as we got better and better. People came early to our games to watch us take crisp infield practice in a professional way. They applauded us as we ran off the field.

We were the best-drilled team in the state and a heavy favorite to win the state championship and advance to the Little League World Series in Williamsport, Pennsylvania. But we lost our final game, 1–0, and were eliminated. I pitched a one-hitter before 3,000 fans. I threw wildly on a bunt single that let in the winning run. After the game, we were presented our runner-up trophies at home plate. When my name was called, the fans applauded, and I began to cry. My uncle walked out to home plate with me with his arm around my shoulder. He was crying, too.

• • • • •

In 1953 my name appeared regularly in headlines in the sports section of the Bridgeport *Post–Telegram.* The stories varied only slightly. Another no-hitter. More strikeouts. My third consecutive no-hitter. My fourth. And so on. I pitched six games that year and gave up only two hits and struck out 110 of the 116 batters I faced. I had been almost perfect. Just two hits all year. In my last two games I struck out every batter I faced, 36 in 12 innings, without allowing a base runner.

After my fourth no-hitter, my parents got a call from a researcher for *Ripley's Believe It or Not.* He wanted to verify certain facts. Possibly I would appear in one of their columns in the Sunday *Parade* magazine. Where, I wondered? Alongside a fat lady who weighed 500 pounds?

A few nights later, we received a call from Dick Young, the *New York Daily News* sportswriter. He interviewed my parents over the phone. Then he interviewed me. A few days later he wrote a column about me, with my photograph alongside it. I was in mid-pitching motion, with a high leg kick and a steely eyed stare of disdain for the invisible batter. Then the Yankees called.

They invited me and my parents to be guests on Mel Allen's pre-game TV show. My parents were thrilled but I took the matter in stride. Already at twelve, I expected that kind of recognition. I wondered what had taken the Yankees so long to call.

We arrived at Yankee Stadium with my parents properly awed and I unimpressed. My mother wore an orchid corsage and my father and I were dressed uncomfortably in suits and ties. We were treated royally. There were pinstripes everywhere. Pictures of Ruth and Gerhig and DiMaggio. My mother swooned. I wondered when they were going to show me to the locker room where I could change into my Yankee uniform. Yankee executives hovered over me, smiling. "So this is our little pitcher. Does he want to be a Yankee when he grows up? I'll bet he's just thrilled to be appearing on television, isn't he?"

Needless to say, I didn't think of myself as a "little pitcher." Nor did I think I had to "grow up" before I could pitch for the Yankees. And finally, the prospect of appearing on television was no big deal for me then because it was a relatively new medium whose full impact was not yet apparent to most people. It was more a novelty than a venue for fame.

If I was thrilled over anything it was the prospect of pitching in front of Casey Steingel, who, I was positive, had invited me to the stadium solely for me to show him and the world "my stuff." That's why I had brought along my glove in a brown paper bag I clutched tightly wherever we were ushered. I expected Mel Allen to turn to me in mid-interview and say, "Pat, why don't you throw a few? Show the fans your stuff." And I would step onto the field, in my brown suit, the camera zooming in close, Casey and the Yankee brass edging closer to me now, everyone expectant. I would begin my wind-up and fire a fastball and the camera man would yell, "Cut!" and tell me in utter amazement that the camera had been unable to record my fastball because the camera couldn't follow it, it was so fast. Would I please throw another, not so fast? And I would. Fastball after fastball that the camera couldn't see until finally the Yankees were so impressed that they signed me to a contract right there, in front of all those astonished viewers. The first twelve-year-old boy ever signed by the Yankees. What an embarrassment it would be for the

CONTINUED ON PAGE 82

Dan Quisenberry

In the mid-'80s, Dan Quisenberry was one of the top relief pitchers in the American League. He was known for his "submarine style" (he pitches from underneath with a low, drop-arm delivery), which I set about capturing in a multiple-exposure picture for *SI's* Baseball Preview Issue.

The multiple-exposure picture, which would break down every part of his pitch, had to be done with a black background. Plus, the editors wanted him pitching from a real mound for a realistic look, so we had to do it after his game in Kansas City one night. The game went long, 10 innings, but Quisenberry was still willing and waited patiently while we took over an hour setting up a huge, 50-foot wall of black velvet behind and around the mound.

When we began running test shots, it was pushing midnight. Quisenberry, my assistant and I realized we were starving, so my assistant called Domino's from the hometeam dugout. The order-taker on the phone asked for the address to which our two large pepperoni and sausage pies should be sent.

"The stadium," my assistant said. The order taker thought it was a prank, but when my assistant gave him the dugout number to call back, he proceeded with our order. My assistant had to go outside through the players' exit and run around to the will-call ticket window to find the Domino's delivery guy. We shared the pizza with the lone maintenance man left in the stadium, the guy who would lock up when Quisenberry, my assistant and I left after eating and making the picture.

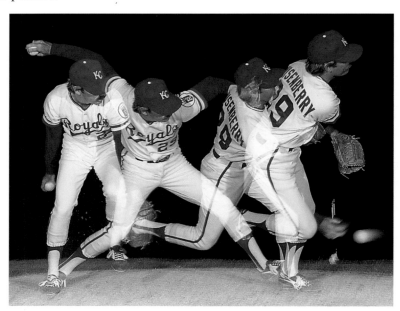

Bob McClure

After almost 19 years in the major leagues as a left-handed pitcher (a jack-of-all-trades, master of none), I think that what the incomparable Bob Uecker, the Milwaukee Brewers announcer, said to me at dinner one night sums up my career best: "Mac," Uecker said, "If you weren't left-handed you'd have been diggin' ditches a long time ago."

Uecker was referring to my height (5'10"), and the velocity of my fastball (a blazing 82–83 mph) not being up to par. He was also alluding to the fact that left-handed pitchers were then and still are a premium; you didn't have to be especially good if you could throw strikes.

What he forgot, though, was that breaking ball — that beautiful, sweeping sidearm-bending junk pitch that seemed to start behind the left-handed hitter to stop and drop at the right time over that gleaming white dish they call home plate. Oh, thank the good Lord for the making of the man who invented the curveball.

"... YOU DIDN'T HAVE TO BE ESPECIALLY GOOD IF YOU COULD THROW STRIKES."

BM

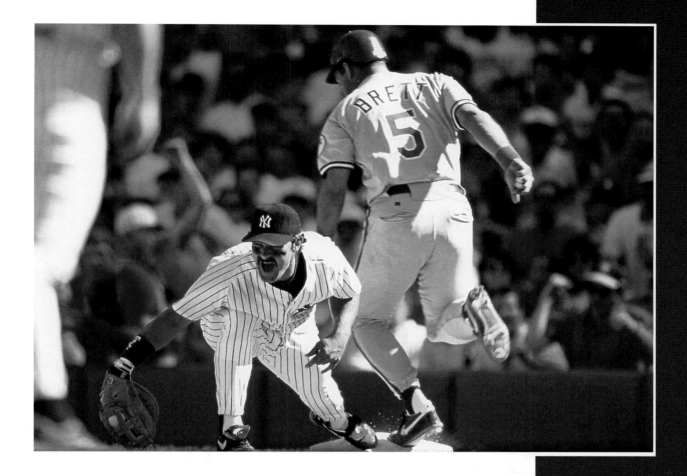

A REFLECTION BY

Don Mattingly

"WHEN YOU'RE
WINNING, EVERY-
ONE IS WILLING
TO SACRIFICE."

DM

Do players today have fun? I believe they still do. But they have to be guarded. If guys have a good time off the field sooner or later it will be in the press. So you become more protective.

You play the game to have a good time. I can't complain about not being in the World Series because a lot of good things happened to me. I was blessed. But it would be a lot better to be able to talk about a World Series. There's a big difference in playing for a team that's playing for a world championship. You have a different attitude. When you're winning, everyone is willing to sacrifice. You're willing to take a walk so the next guy can drive in a run. You're stronger in every direction. But when you're playing on a team going through some lean years, it's not as enjoyable. There's more selfishness in the lockeroom.

It was totally my choice to retire, and fortunately the Yankees were great with me. I wasn't ready to make the decision on retirement right away so the Yankees gave me a little time. I was treated with a lot of respect by Mr. Steinbrenner.

Yankees' pitcher, Vic Raschi. How he would envy me, throwing in my suit and tie with more speed than he ever dreamed of.

Before the interview, I went into the Yankees' dugout and met Casey Steingel. It didn't surprise me that he'd heard of me. "All dem strikeouts," he said. "Sonny, I guess your fielders don't need no gloves when you pitch." I nodded seriously.

We were seated in box seats along the third-base line. Cameras were aimed at us from the field. The signal was given. Mel Allen, turning to his right, asked my parents a question. My father fidgeted. My mother touched her corsage. One of them answered. More questions. Nervous smiles. Quick glances at the camera then back to Mel. I sat at the end of the row, farthest from the camera. I could barely hear them, but it did not matter. I just sat there, waiting, my heart pounding, the brown bag at my feet. And when it was almost

DWIGHT GOODEN
NEW YORK CITY, 1991

over, and Casey and the brass had not appeared, and I knew it was too late for me to throw because Raschi was already on the mound, Mel turned to me and leaned across my parents to ask me a question. His lips peeled apart like an open wound. I was so disheartened I could not answer. He repeated his question. I mumbled something. The camera panned in close. Mel said something. I glared across the field at Vic Raschi, warming up with his pathetic fastball!

"Cut!"

• • • • •

I never did pitch for the Yankees. After I graduated from high school I signed a $50,000 bonus contract with the then Milwaukee Braves and went off to the minor leagues to pursue my career. It didn't last long. Three years of diminishing success and then I was out, back home in Connecticut to begin my ordinary life.

It was August of 1962, the year I left baseball — the phrase I always use although it is not quite accurate. Baseball left me. I was married and needed a job. I got one, as a laborer for a stone mason. He hired me reluctantly, he said, "Because athletes are too soft for this work." I guess I proved him right. He fired me after a month.

I was so disheartened by my failure at such a "menial" job that I couldn't bear to look for another. I had thought, romantically, that baseball would be the one great failure of my life. Now it was dawning on me that baseball was merely the first of many such failures in my adult life, and I was only was 21 years old.

I could think of nothing to do now, nothing that really mattered to me, so I decided to do again the only thing that ever mattered. I decided to pitch. To make a comeback. To see if I couldn't catch on with another team's minor league organization.

I began throwing from a bag of baseballs into the home-plate screen at the park where I first played baseball as an eight-year-old boy. I jogged after the balls lying around home plate, returned to the mound, and threw again. It soothed me. The pump, the kick, the follow-through. After a week of throwing I felt it coming back, the speed, the good overhand curve, the confidence. It wasn't too late, I thought. After all, I was only 21. I still had time. It would be easy. I'd throw on my own for a few weeks, then I'd call up some high-school catcher who'd be only too happy to catch an ex-minor-leaguer like me. Then after a few more weeks of throwing, watching his eyes light up when I cut loose a fastball, I'd call up some manager in the Senior City League, where at fifteen I had pitched a no-hitter in my first game, and struck out fourteen. He'd jump at the chance

CONTINUED ON PAGE 86

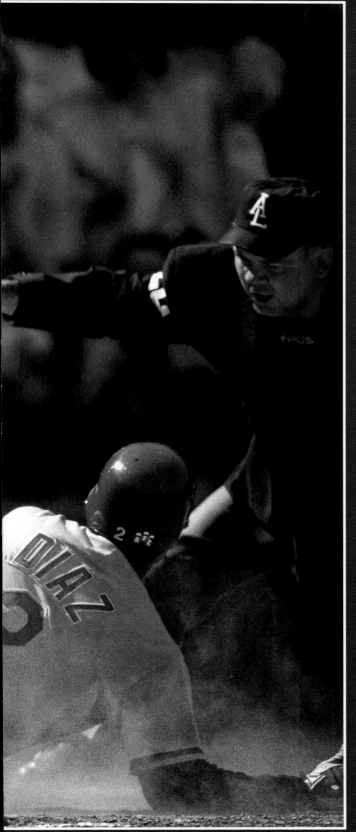

TONY PEÑA
FENWAY PARK, BOSTON, 1990

RICKY HENDERSON
OAKLAND COLISEUM, 1982

to pitch me a few games. He'd probably offer me some money. A hundred dollars a game. Or maybe fifty. Then after a few nice games, four-hitters, maybe ten strikeouts, the scouts would begin to come around again. I'd know them this time. We'd swap stories before a game, minor league stories, players they'd signed and I knew, inside stuff, who was drinking too much, who was hurt, and then we'd get down to it. You're throwing good yourself, they'd say. Not bad, I'd say. Then one or more of them would make me an offer. Not a bonus like before. (I'd been given $50,000 by the Braves in 1959.) Not a big bonus, anyway. Maybe just a few thousand, to show good faith. And I'd be back where I belonged, in the minor leagues, fulfilling my destiny.

But first I had to muster the courage to even go *see* a Senior City League game. I had been so ashamed of my failure that I couldn't bear to show my face at any of the parks in town where I'd had my youthful successes. I feared the inevitable questions. "What happened?" I still didn't know. I knew only that I had left to play minor league baseball on a cloud of expectations and then, three years later, I was dumped, unceremoniously, in the dust. Dazed. Uncomprehending.

Finally, one weekday evening, I drove to Seaside Park in Bridgeport near Long Island Sound. I stood behind a huge tree along the first-base line. Hid behind it, really. Watching the players arrive. Most SCL games were played at twilight. The players rushed to the park from their real jobs as carpenters, masons, and factory machinists, only minutes before the games began. They changed into their uniforms in their cars and took the field without warming up — they had no careers to protect — looking so odd with their chalky white hands dusted with lime.

SCL games were not like the Babe Ruth and high-school games of my youth. Young boys with high-stirruped stockings playing in cool, green suburbs before polite crowds of their parents and teen-aged girls on ten-speed bikes. These were city games, played after work in the heat, before a crowd of blacks and Puerto Ricans and old men drinking out of paper bags, and even older men, ex-players, who now stood only a few feet away from me. These old-timers were tough on the players on the field, who, no matter how gritty a game they played, were never as tough, in those old men's minds, as the players they remembered from their youth. Each generation, it

CONTINUED ON PAGE 93

CARLTON FISK - CHICAGO, 1990

Nolan Ryan

In 1986, Nolan Ryan was pitching no-hitters for the Houston Astros and running two cattle ranches in his "spare time." I was assigned to capture both jobs for *Sports Illustrated.* When logistics posed a problem (Ryan had only one day off between games), I hired a helicopter to transport him from his suburban front lawn in Alvin, Texas, to his ranch in Gonzalez, Texas.

Ryan, my assistant and I boarded the helicopter in Alvin. As we were taking off, the windows fogged up completely. Everyone stopped talking. My blood pressure soared. My assistant looked pale. Ryan looked cool and confidant, but still remained silent.

"I can just see the newspaper headline," I said. "Nolan Ryan dies in helicopter crash. Also killed were two other guys and the pilot." My assistant and Ryan laughed. Even the pilot managed a grin, since he was succeeding in beginning to defog his windows.

We landed safely and immediately followed Ryan, who was on horseback, to a cluster of cattle. He roped a few of them. Then swept them back and forth. Closed a gate for us. Then we returned to the waiting helicopter and flew back to Alvin so Ryan could rest before the next day's game.

"EVERYONE STOPPED TALKING. MY BLOOD PRESSURE SOARED. MY ASSISTANT LOOKED PALE. RYAN LOOKED COOL AND CONFIDENT, BUT STILL REMAINED SILENT."

RCM

A REFLECTION BY

Johnny Bench

One of the best times in my life was when I broke Yogi Berra's home run record in 1980. What made it even sweeter was the telegram I received from Berra himself on that occasion. The telegram read:

> Johnny: Congratulations on breaking my home run record last night. I always thought the record would stand until it was broken. It couldn't have happened to a nicer guy. Best of luck the rest of the season, but take it easy on Dale and the Pirates. Maybe we'll see you in October.
>
> — Yogi (July 16, 1980)

JOHNNY BENCH

FRANK WHITE - KANSAS CITY ROYALS
ROYALS STADIUM, 1979

seemed, was weaker than the last.

The players in those SCL games were in their late twenties, thirties, forties, even. They had once been prospects, had maybe even gone away to the minor leagues before getting released. Some were even in their fifties, like big Al Bike, a mean-looking, barrel-chested catcher, and Rufus Baker, a lean, trim black man with gray hair. Some of the players had even made the major leagues for a brief spell, like Tom Casagrande. Tommy "Big House," 6'3"and 235 pounds. A huge, red-headed, freckle-faced, southpaw pitcher with a smooth, effortless motion. His meaty arms were freckled and dusted with orange hair, like down. Tom was my idol when I was a kid. He had pitched a few years with the Phillies and Robin Roberts before he drifted back to the SCL, where he still threw good — good enough to get those batters out anyway.

Some of the players, like Bill Onuska, a catcher, had come so close to the major leagues they could taste it, but never did. Bill caught in Triple-A for years without being called up to the majors, and finally, in his thirties, quit, and returned to the SCL. I was a senior in high school when I heard he had returned home. It was mid-winter. I called him up, introduced myself. He said he'd heard of me. I asked him if he'd catch me at the boys club gym, teach me a few things. He agreed. I said I'd pay him ten dollars a work-out. We met there one cold night. I began to throw to him on the side of the court while kids played basketball. After about five minutes I cut loose with a fastball. Bill caught it and bounced out of this crouch. He walked toward me. He reached into his back pocket for the ten-dollar bill I'd given him. He handed it to me.

"Here, kid," he said. "You don't need me."

There were other SCL stars I remembered, too, like Dick Grassia, a slick-fielding third-baseman, who had been offered a number of minor league contracts but turned them all down because of his band. The band was "Dick Grass and the Hoppers," a fifties rock n' roll band that made it briefly to the bottom of the charts with their rendition of "Mr. John Law."

I was only a kid when I pitched in the SCL. A fifteen-year-old sophomore in high school. I struck out SCL batters at will then. I struck out thirty-year-old ex-minor-leaguers like Nicky Vancho and Vinny Corda and Ronnie "The Globe" DelBianco, and they didn't like it much. They shouted at me on the mound after they swung

CONTINUED ON PAGE 96

KENNY LOFTON - ATLANTA BRAVES
HOUSTON ASTRODOME, 1997

CRAIG NETTLES
NEW YORK YANKEES, 1980

through their third strike. "You bastard! I'll get you next time." But they didn't.

I'd walk off the field at the end of the innings and my first-baseman would meet me as we crossed the foul line. "Nice throwing, son," he'd say. He was a meticulous man with neat, short hair and a placid nature — Whitey McCall. He never swore like the other players. Whitey McCall, Father John McCall, a Catholic parish priest.

As I stood under that big tree, watching the game unfold, I grew excited at the thought of being a part of it again. How, now, all the older guys on the field would treat me as an equal, not a kid, because I had taken my lumps, like they had, in the minor leagues. Maybe, too, I would bring my young wife to my games now, like they did. The wives standing off together, chattering absentmindedly, rocking baby carriages, glad to be out of their third-floor, un-air-conditioned walk-up apartments in the city for even a few hours.

Suddenly I heard my name. It came from the old-timers standing only a few feet in front of me. I caught a breath. They stood there, a cluster of wizened magpies, bachelors all, little old ladies, really, with nothing to do in their lives except carp about young players.

"Jordan's back," one of them said.

"Figures," said another. There was a clucking of tongues and a shaking of heads.

"I knew he'd never make it," said a third.

I felt weak-kneed, light-headed. I had to wait a bit before I walked back to my car. I hoped no one would see me. I got in my car and drove off. I never did come back. I didn't pick up a baseball again for 35 years. I put baseball out of my mind, gave up the illusion of it as a game that would always be a part of my life, and pursued my ordinary life, had children, taught high-school English, worked on a newspaper, became a freelance writer, wrote a book about my minor league years, distanced myself from the game I'd loved. Until suddenly, one day, it all came back to me, by accident.

• • • • •

For almost ten years I couldn't bear to watch a major league game on television. All I would see were players I had played with, or against, who were having long major league careers. Phil Niekro, Joe Torre, Ron Hunt, Tony Cloninger. I began to rationalize that I wouldn't want to be living their lives, except on the playing field. I always loved to play the game. But life off the field — the travel, the hotel rooms on the road, the absences from families. The locker room. They were forced to spend their days and nights with 24 other men, with whom they often had little in common. I, on the other hand, picked and chose my friends. I grew a beard, without worrying about team rules. I spent time with my growing family, a wife and five children. I lived my own life, any way I wanted to. Niekro and Torre and Hunt, I rationalized, were trapped in a way I wasn't. It was only the game they had, and the money, that I didn't. But I had so many more things that they were forced to live without. Freedom, mainly. Then in my thirties, I became friendly with Tom Seaver and discovered the one thing I was really missing, and had overlooked.

Tom and I became friends. Not the best of friends. Not intimate friends. Just casual friends. I used to call him now and then when he was pitching badly. If he wasn't home, I'd call him back. "You know Thomas," his wife, Nancy, said. "He never returns calls." Sometimes I'd catch him at home.

"Tom. It's me."

"What do you want?"

"I saw you last night on the tube. Against the Reds."

"And . . ."

"You're throwing too many curveballs."

"You think so?"

"Yep."

"What the hell do you know?"

We used to play basketball in the winter at the YMCA in Greenwich, Connecticut, where Tom lived. One-on-one in a deserted gym. Two big guys banging away at each other pretty good. The walls echoed with the thud of flesh against flesh. There was a brick wall close to the basket so we had to watch ourselves at first. We'd drive to the hoop, shoot, and then raise our hands, palms out, to cushion the shock when we hit the wall.

One day Tom had the ball close to the hoop. He faked. I went up. As I came down, he went up, his shoulder clipping my jaw, rattling my senses, and scored.

"You all right?" he said, without interest. He walked back to half-court with the ball.

"Sure." I smiled at him. When his back was turned I opened my mouth and moved my jaw around to see if it was still attached.

We had been playing for hours. We were both drenched with sweat, our faces red and swollen from exhaustion and our fierce competition. Tom was only an adequate basketball player. Strong,

CONTINUED ON PAGE 102

Mickey Mantle

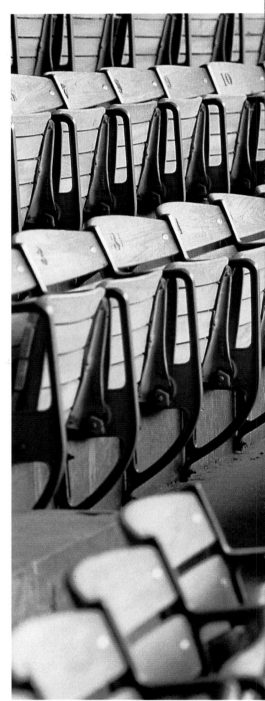

One humid summer morning during the mid-'80s, I went to the Braves/Expos spring training stadium in West Palm Beach, Florida. I was working on the stills for an instructional video that Mickey Mantle was filming with Tom Seaver and Gary Carter. It was the second day of the shoot and I had arrived very early.

I walked into the stadium and looked around. There was a lone figure sitting in one of the seats, about halfway up the lower grandstand on the third-base side. He was the only person in the whole stadium. He was an older man in a plain gray baseball uniform and cap. He had one elbow on each knee and he rested his chin on his clasped hands while he stared at the empty field.

It was Mickey Mantle.

I walked up the stairs toward him. He nodded at me.

"What's going on today?" I asked.

"Oh, I'm just sitting here thinking," he said, "God I wish I could still play."

ROBIN YOUNT

A REFLECTION BY

Robin Yount

It was easier for me to fit in the big leagues at 18 because I had an older brother who played professional baseball. I used to spend a few weeks in the summer in Triple-A with him. I lived the professional baseball lifestyle. I worked out with Triple-A players so I already knew what to expect at 15. For some guys it must be a shock to their system if they don't know what they're getting into. They're just thrown out on their own. But I was treated very well with Milwaukee. No one gave me a hard time. There were just a lot of jokes.

The fun of being in the big leagues wore off very quickly. As a young player you have to learn to stick with what got you there. It's a mistake to think you can't do in the big leagues what you did before you got there. It was a blessing early on to be with a losing team. That's the only reason I got a chance to play at 18. Milwaukee was an expansion team with little or no chance at success. If I was with an organization that had past successes I probably wouldn't have gotten a chance to play. Still, it was frustrating to play with a team that finished at the bottom every year. At times I questioned myself. Do I want to do this? Because losing was a new experience.

straight moves. Without grace. Clumsy, in fact, which was to his advantage. It excused his blatant fouls. But he had strong hands, and once he got close to the hoop he was unstoppable. His basic move was to back in to the hoop, left–right–left–right, until he was close enough to throw up a short jump shot. Even with me hanging on his arms, he was strong enough to put the ball in. But I was a better shooter. Tom would get furious when I would dribble the ball nonchalantly at the top of the key and suddenly go up for a long jump shot. Swish! When I tried to get close to the hoop, he'd slow me down with a shoulder to the gut. But then, I did the same to him. When he went up for a jump shot I'd time my jump and slap the ball back into his face. The ball bounced right into the air. Without wiping the blood from his nose, Tom snared the ball and went up again, this time with the top of his head aimed at my jaw. Clunk. I backpedaled. Swish. He grinned. Blood trickled down his nose.

"You all right?" he said.

"Sure. Want me to get some tissue for your nose?" He glared at me.

We went on like this for hours. He won a game. I won a game. Finally, after too many games to count, we agreed that the winner of the last game would win the day. By this time we were both bruised and scraped, our T-shirts speckled with blood. Our knees and elbows were raw. There was a pulsating welt on my forehead. Tom's nose was swollen like a pig's.

The game was tied and the next basket would win. Tom had the ball at the top of the key. He was dribbling around to catch his breath. I was crouched over, panting like a rabid dog, waiting for him to begin backing in to the hoop. But he surprised me. Suddenly he took a dribble and drove straight to the basket. Just as he was about to go up for a basket I was about to push him with both hands. Then I saw the wall in front of him, and in my mind's eye, I saw him slamming into that wall, heard the sickening sound of his arm breaking, *crack,* against the bricks. Tom Seaver's arm! Jesus! I dropped my hands and let him score.

It was raining outside as we drove back to Tom's house in my old Corvette with the T-top roof that rattled and leaked. It was painted gold.

"Nice color," Tom said, laughing. "Why didn't you buy a Porsche?"

I looked across at him. "Because I'm not Tom Seaver."

"That's a fact." Rain seeped through the T-top roof and dropped on Tom's brow. "It leaks."

"No shit." I was hunched over the steering wheel, wiping off the fogged-up windows.

"Put on the defroster." I glared at him. "That too!" He laughed in his high-pitched, girlish voice.

"You know I let you win that last game," I said, to piss him off.

"You did, huh?"

"Yeah. I was afraid if I pushed you into the wall I'd break your arm."

He looked over at me, his eyebrows raised, with a faint smile. "Bullshit! You never let anyone win at anything in your life."

"Usually true. But not today. I mean, you're Tom Seaver, a big fucking star pitcher. I coulda broke your arm." He didn't answer. "You know what else? I threw harder than you, too."

"In your dreams."

"No, really, Tom. I did. I just didn't know where the ball was

CONTINUED ON PAGE 106

MILWAUKEE BREWERS
VS. TORONTO BLUE JAYS,
1974

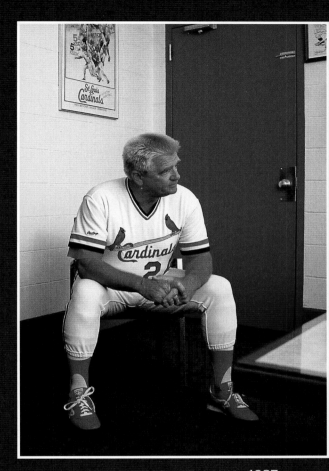

WHITEY HERZOG - ST. LOUIS, 1987

"FRED BIRD"
BUSCH STADIUM, ST. LOUIS, 1987

going." We both laughed.

It had stopped raining when we reached his house. He lighted a barbecue grill and prepared the steaks for our lunch on the front porch. We talked pitching, what kind of year he was having, how his arm felt, stuff like that. Soon Nancy joined us. She told stories about Tom. Cute stories meant to poke fun at him as if he was a precocious child we were both fawning over.

It did not bother Tom to be talked about in the third person. Thomas this. Thomas that. Nancy and I laughed. Tom grilled the steaks. Nancy and I looked at him. Tom was used to this kind of attention. Being the focus of attention. Always. He accepted it as his due for being a famous athlete. It's what I really missed, I realized, when I left baseball. Being the object, always, of everybody's attention. Tom still had what I lost, the greatest loss for an athlete no longer playing the game. An Athlete's Blessing.

Tom and I were friends for a few years and then drifted apart. In all those years, we never had a conversation about anything other than him, his pitching, his life, his salary squabbles. Imagine, he'd say, the Mets only offered him $300,000, not the $400,000 he deserved. I felt bad for him. "How do they expect me to live?" he shrieked. At the time I supported a wife and five children on less than $15,000 a year, but Tom never knew this. He never asked. He never asked what my ambitions were, how my writing was going. He talked only about himself. He expected the conversation only to be about him. It was his Athlete's Blessing. His problems were more real than mine. His life was so much bigger than mine. A non-athlete's life and problems are unreal to famous athletes. When Tom asked why I didn't swap in my ratty 'Vette for a Porsche, he was serious. *He* would have. In his world, my refusal to do so was not an example of diminished circumstances, but willful obstinacy. If I was driving to the hoop for that winning basket, *he* would have pushed me into the wall.

• • • • •

It all began as a joke. I had written a story about the St. Paul Saints of the Independent Northern League in the summer of '96. The Northern League was a league for men with a past but not much of a future. Players who had got old, or injured, or were burdened

CONTINUED ON PAGE 113

DENNIS MARTINEZ - MONTREAL EXPOS
WEST PALM BEACH, 1993

". . . HE WENT
FOUR-FOR-FOUR
ONE NIGHT.
HE DECIDED
IT MUST HAVE
BEEN SOMETHING
HE ATE."

RCM

Wade Boggs

Baseball players are among the most superstitious of men. Show me a team on a winning streak and I'll show you a team of men who haven't changed their underwear in a week.

When Wade Boggs was playing in the minor leagues, he went four-for-four one night. He decided it must have been something he ate. So the chicken he had eaten for dinner before the game got all the credit.

Boggs proclaimed he would eat nothing but chicken from that day forward. His poultry preference became legendary in baseball circles. He even put out a chicken cookbook. So, in 1986 when *SI* was featuring Boggs (now a Boston Red Sox star) in the Baseball Preview issue, it was decided he should be photographed with a bunch of chickens.

I found Boggs at the Red Sox spring training camp in Winterhaven. He agreed to the chicken shot. We picked him up to drive to the chicken ranch. What I didn't tell him, because I feared he might nix the shoot, was how far away the ranch was (over an hour's drive). So I gave him a bottle of Dom Perignon champagne before I told him. I'd hoped he would be so busy thinking of what to serve with the champagne (chicken cordon bleu?) that he might relax. He did.

Boggs was great, he really hammed it up. The place stunk so we tried to work quickly. It was hard, though, because every time a flash went off, the chickens pulled their heads back into their cages. We had to wait for them to recover and stick their heads out again.

Then the ranch manager came in and asked us to finish. He was concerned that the flashes would upset the hens' egg-laying. So we quit and went to lunch. We all had chicken.

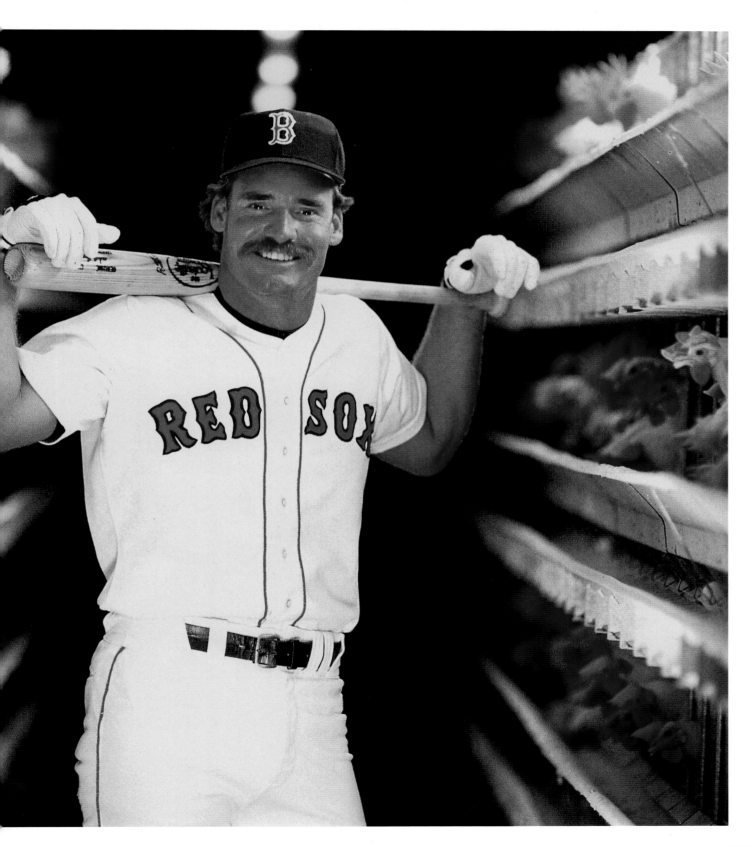

BENITO SANTIAGO - SAN DIEGO PADRES
YUMA, ARIZONA, 1989

Bob Uecker

How lucky can one guy be?

I'm living a dream. Not too many people can say that. That's why I'm thankful, each and every day, that I've had the privilege to be around this game. I love baseball and everything and everybody associated with it.

To be born and raised in Milwaukee, and play professionally there, was a big kick. Then, I was fortunate to be able to return and broadcast big league baseball there.

I know what it's like to lose. I know what it's like to be a winner. I played on a world championship team, and the next year we'd finish near the bottom of the standings. I know what it's like to get your fanny kicked. I know what it's like to kick some fanny. The happiness in the clubhouse; the doldrums; you learn a lot about this game. You learn a lot about life.

I also respect the guys in this business. Guys that broadcast for poor clubs — clubs that lose season after season after season — they know how to broadcast. They have to keep the game interesting for the fans. I appreciate those guys more. They keep fans listening. That's the real challenge of keeping fans tuned in.

I've had so many great times in this game. Someday, I know this will end for me. I can honestly say, if this were to end for me tomorrow, I'd have no regrets.

It's not only what you see on the field that matters. It's the people who come out to the ball park every day. It's the people that make this game great. I try not to forget that.

A REFLECTION BY

Bob Costas

Here's a problem with baseball: Everybody's so fit and buffed now, that there's no place for a Roger Freed.

Roger Freed was one of my favorite players ever. A guy who looked like the clean-up man in a beer league. A guy who tore the minors apart, but got only 717 at-bats in parts of eight big league seasons. But one of his 27 major league home runs came in the most dramatic of possible circumstances.

May 1, 1979; bottom of the 11th at Busch Stadium. Houston: 6, St. Louis: 3. Bases loaded, two out. Lefty Joe Sambito, the nearly invincible relief ace, looking to finish it for the Astros. Up steps our man, Freed, to pinch hit. I guess you can figure out what he did. I still remember the crack of the bat, and the split-second of disbelieving silence that preceded the happy roar for this Everyman's greatest moment.

Soon after that, Roger Freed was gone from baseball. He died in 1996. He was just 49. For the last seventeen years of his life, I'll bet there weren't many days when he didn't recall that swing. That tour of the bases. The sound of that crowd. That night.

DARRYL STRAWBERRY - LA DODGERS
SAN DIEGO, CALIFORNIA, 1991

with bad reputations as druggies or drinkers or just plain malcontents. It was a league that gave players a second chance when organized teams with major league affiliations wouldn't. The owner of the Saints was Mike Veech, son of the famous baseball owner, Bill Veech. Mike and I became friendly that summer and when I began to write the story in the fall I'd call him up every so often to check my facts. We'd talk, about nothing really, just baseball, two men who always loved the game. One day I saw in the *Miami Herald* that the actor, Charlie Sheen, had signed a contract to pitch for the Saints. I thought there might be a story in it for me, so I called Mike. I approached the subject obliquely, the way wise guys and jocks do.

"So," I said, "I hear Charlie Sheen's gonna pitch for you, Mike?"

"Yeah."

"Jeez, Mike. If that fucking actor thinks he can pitch so can I."

"You serious?"

I wasn't serious. I hadn't even thought about what I'd said. But I couldn't resist being the wise guy. "Shit, yes, I'm serious."

"Then get in shape. I'll pitch you."

So there it was. I had trapped myself into pitching again for the first time in 35 years. I had always subconsciously harbored the desire to pitch again all these years but I'd never had the impetus. Now I did. At 56. An old man with a white beard, who, no matter how old he'd become, had always seen himself not as a writer, but as a pitcher who happened to be writing. Writing was what I did. Pitching was what I am.

I began to throw in January for the June season. I threw three times a week into a home-plate screen by myself until I thought I was throwing well enough to get a catcher. I found a high-school shortstop who was willing to catch me. His name was Brian LaBasco. I threw to him three times a week for three months until I thought I was ready to pitch in a minor league game. During those months I learned that Mike had signed a woman, Ila Borders, to pitch for the Saints. Now, when I called him, he seemed less than enthusiastic to have me pitch for him. I realized he thought he couldn't have three novelties on the Saints — a woman, an actor, and an old man — so I searched around for another team that would pitch me. I found Bob Wirsz, owner of the Waterbury, Connecticut Spirit of the Independent Northeast League. He agreed to pitch me for one inning under one condition.

CONTINUED ON PAGE 116

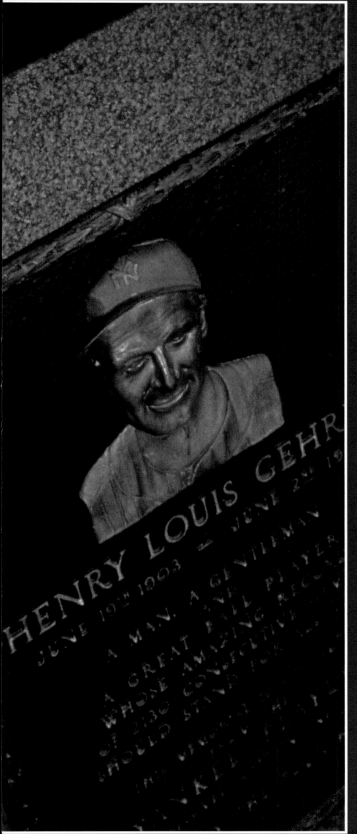

STEVE HOWE
WORLD SERIES, YANKEE STADIUM, 1981

CAL RIPKIN, JR.
YANKEE STADIUM, NEW YORK, 1990

"This better not be a joke," he said over the phone.

I assured him I had no intention of making a fool myself on the mound a second time. And I didn't. I took the mound for the first time in 35 years on July 29, 1997. It's funny. I was nervous at first, but then, after two pitches, fastballs off the plate, I forgot about being nervous and concentrated only on getting this batter out. I almost immediately became a pitcher again. With 2–0 on the batter, I knew he was guessing a fastball. So I threw him a slider down the middle. He swung just as it broke away from his bat. He hit a weak grounder to short for the first out. I walked the next batter, then got the third batter to ground weakly to first base for the second out. I threw the fourth hitter two fastballs up and in for strikes. Then I struck him out swinging on a devastating slider. I walked off the mound to the sound of applause in a daze. It had all been so easy. What had I been afraid of? I had been right after all. I was still a pitcher.

Immediately after the game I was interviewed by reporters. They wanted to know why I did it. I, myself, wasn't sure why I did it at the time. I thought maybe I did it to exorcise the demons of my failure. Or maybe I was just an old man trying to recapture lost youth. Maybe I just did it to get batters out, to be a pitcher. Or maybe just to see the baseball spin through the air in a way that always pleased me. God, how I loved to throw a baseball. It was the first distinction I ever had as a young boy in Little League. It defined me then, and, in my mind's eye, always has. Baseball has always been such a big part of my life that even during the 35 years I had turned my back on it, it was still there, waiting patiently for me to turn around and acknowledge its place in my life just like a faithful dog. So I did.

I am still throwing baseballs into home-plate screens as I write this. I plan to pitch a full season for The Spirits in 1998. The owner of the team, Bob Wirsz, asked me how long I thought I could last in a game, a season. I said, "Until the batters tell me it's time to get off the mound." A simple rule of thumb.

THE END

RANDY JOHNSON
MONTREAL EXPOS, 1989

STEVE CARLTON
VETERAN STADIUM, PHILADELPHIA, 1984

YANKEES' JUBILATION AFTER WORLD SERIES
YANKEE STADIUM, NEW YORK, 1996

Rod Carew

Rod Carew was the first major star I photographed one-on-one. When I was the Brewers' team photographer I had shot Carew in action, but when Rick Cerone, then publisher of *Baseball Magazine* (and later Yankees PR director), assigned me to shoot a portrait of Carew, I knew I wanted to do something special.

Carew was the second-baseman for the Minnesota Twins. He was already a four-time batting champion bound for the Hall of Fame. I could have hooked up with him when the Twins came to Milwaukee, but I wanted to photograph him in his home uniform.

So I drove to Minneapolis and went to meet him at the yard. I was nervous about approaching him. I waited until none of his teammates were around. Carew recognized me from Milwaukee and put me immediately at ease. "What are you doing up here?" he asked.

I told him about wanting to photograph him in his home uniform. He laughed. "You drove all the way from Milwaukee for that?"

He suggested doing the portrait right away. He was patient, making suggestions, asking me if there was anything else I needed. *Baseball Magazine* ran an action cover and a nice, available-light portrait inside.

The next time the Twins came to Milwaukee, Carew approached me on the field. He asked me about my equipment and said he always kept a camera with him. "I like to photograph my teammates," he said.

Every time we saw each other over the years we would talk about photography. Mostly about why sports photographers use such long lenses. I'd let him look through my 600 mm lens. I'd give him some film. Later, Carew got into landscapes. *SI* even published some of his work in the early 80s.

Now a batting coach for the California Angels, Carew is still shooting. I'm glad he does mostly landscapes. With every ex-lawyer, restaurateur and friend of a photographer buying autofocus lenses, there's more than enough competition around.

"EVERY TIME
WE SAW
EACH OTHER
OVER THE YEARS
WE WOULD
TALK ABOUT
PHOTOGRAPHY."

RCM

A REFLECTION BY

Tom Glavine

The hardest time for me was during and right after the strike [in '94]. I was the Braves players' rep and I ended up on TV a lot, giving the players' point of view. The fans didn't understand what the strike was about. They thought it was all about a bunch of rich guys wanting more money. But there were lots of other issues.

Since I was out front, they hated me for it.

When we started playing again, I would get booed out on the mound. It seemed like if I had a bad game, people were happy. Then it died down, after time. I'm not angry anymore, but the resentment is still there.

Would I do it again? I'd have to say yes. If you believe in something, you've got to fight for it.

A   R E F L E C T I O N   B Y
Eric Davis

It's been a tough ordeal, but I'm no Superman. I already knew what it was like to face life without baseball. I did it in 1985 when I retired after neck surgery. I've always had a good rapport with the people, but I never knew about love and support like this.

Life is too short to worry about anything. You had better enjoy it because the next day promises nothing. People spend time worrying about things they think they have to have and lose perception of what they do have. You can have all the money and material things you want. If you aren't here to enjoy them, what good do they do?

I'm having a good time. I'm going to treat every game and every day as if they are my last because I now know that they could be.

[Re: His battle with cancer, which appears to be in remission]

DAN GLADDEN AND GREG OLSON, 1991

JEFF BLAUSER AND DARREN DAULTON
FULTON COUNTY STADIUM, ATLANTA, 1993

The Japan Series

W hen the 1994 World Series was canceled in the United States due to the major league baseball players' strike, *SI* sent me to Japan so baseball-starved Americans could have a baseball cover story for the first time in weeks.

Japanese baseball players tend to behave themselves. They definitely don't strike. So I knew if I took the 18-hour flight to Japan and took a $225 cab ride from the airport to the Tokyo Dome, I would find baseball. And I did. But getting in position to photograph was not that simple.

In Japan, only newspaper photographers are allowed on the field. Magazine photographers pay to sit in the stands. So we bought four seats behind home plate for 200,000 yen ($2,000 in 1994) but the view was obstructed by a big black net. I needed to be at ground level. It took several days, then several hours on game day to convince our Japanese hosts it would be a great honor to give me a photo position on the field.

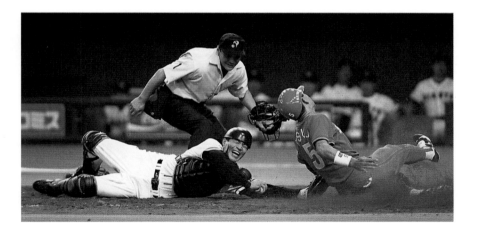

American sportswriters tend to wax poetic about the symmetry and orderliness of baseball. Japanese baseball makes our version of the game look like South-central L.A. during the riots. Japanese fans pass their trash to the end of the row. Their cheers are rehearsed chants between plays. Spontaneous outbursts of applause are rare.

At the conclusion of every Japan Series, the victorious team gathers in a cluster around the pitcher's mound, collects their manager, then tosses him into the air three times. I wish I could say I made this photograph by following the energy of the game. By instinct. But I didn't. After the final pitch was thrown, I swung my lens to the mound and kept it there. I knew what was coming.

Spontaneous, no. But the joy on the Giants' faces looked real to me.

> "ONCE THE GAME
> IS TAKEN AWAY
> FROM YOU,
> YOU REALLY
> MISS IT."
>
> GC

A REFLECTION BY

Gary Carter

Growing up it was my dream to play in the major leagues. But I never thought the money would get to where it is today. I wanted to be in the big leagues by the time I turned 20 and be making $100,000 by 25.

I always thought of baseball as just a sport I loved. Baseball gave me everything, opportunities, financial security and a chance to meet interesting people. Once the game is taken away from you, you really miss it. No matter how old you get, you're still a kid at heart. I missed the camaraderie when I retired. A lot of guys go through major depressions once they go back to normal life. What hurt me the most was that when I became a broadcaster the players didn't treat me the same anymore. I felt I was different now. An outsider. Not a part of it anymore. Especially when I was with the Marlins.

Now with the Expos, I've got my own locker, my own uniform, and I throw batting practice. I feel like one of the guys again.

The greatest thing about the game is to face Goose Gossage with the game on the line. No drug can replace that feeling.

What it is is the game.

GARY CARTER

Kirk Gibson

In the eighties, David Letterman had a character on his show he called "Gruff-but-Lovable Gus" who drove the *Late Night* bookmobile. That's how I've always thought of Kirk Gibson. Not as a guy driving a bookmobile. But as Gruff-but-Lovable.

"Gibby" put on a growly show. He was a tough player. When I saw him rounding third I knew there was going to be a collision at the plate. And a great picture.

One-on-one he could be tough, too. Especially with photographers. Once, as he took batting practice while several photographers shot in his direction, he growled: "Get those cameras out of my face! That's the only guy who can take my picture!"

He was pointing at me. I was leaning against the wall, not shooting. I wasn't sure if he meant that as a joke since I wasn't shooting or if he really meant it. In any case, Gibby always treated me well. Maybe because we were both from the Midwest (he's from Michigan) and liked to hunt and fish. Several times he whipped out pictures of himself with his kids gathered around a deer they'd shot.

"Now there's a picture," he'd say.

In 1991, I began working on a series of portraits for Topps Chewing Gum. While working in Chicago one day I approached Gibby to do his portrait.

"Oh," he groused, "you know I hate doing this bullshit. Where do you want me?"

We went to the batting cage where I shot off about forty snaps . . . then I froze. I tried to be nonchalant about motioning to my assistant but Gibby was alert.

"Big Mr. *Sports Illustrated* forgot to put film in his camera," he roared.

At least he seemed at ease during the rest of the shoot.

A REFLECTION BY

Keith Hernandez

The Mets of the 70s struck a chord with fans, either positive or negative. We were arrogant and cocky with a lot of personality you don't see today. Today's players are more corporate-like — they're boring, like IBM executives. They're more protected today. But maybe rightly so because they're more aware of the press.

When I played in St. Louis, it was a provincial city and the fans didn't give a shit what we did off the field. In New York it was more difficult. We got a lot of attention from the fans and the press. They had no patience with kids just coming up in the league. In St. Louis, when I came up at 21, the fans were supportive. I was so fragile at the time, I don't know if I could have cut it in New York as a 21-year-old. New York is a tough place to make it. There's just as much temptation in other cities as in New York, it's just that in other cities, the fans and the press don't dig into your personal life.

A REFLECTION BY
Willie Stargell

The day I was inducted into the Hall of Fame in 1988, I just can't describe the feeling. No word has been invented to describe it. It was like nothing you could ever experience. Here I was, on the podium with all these living legends. It was a humbling effect for sure. Then when they announced my name I had trouble just getting up from my chair. I was so nervous! I had to stand with my feet apart to keep my knees from knocking together!

I was honored and proud. I mean, it was my dream as a kid to be a Major League player. But getting in the Hall of Fame, you just think it would never happen. It blows your mind. You think about people who had a tremendous impact on the game. Then you are one of them!

To this day, it's still sinking in. Sometimes I need to pinch myself.

SCOTT BROSIUS - OAKLAND A'S
MILWAUKEE COUNTY STADIUM, 1997

Goose Gossage

When they went on strike in 1994, most players knew their season was over. But pitching legend Goose Gossage, the one player who had been around for all the major league baseball work stoppages, feared his career might be over. A career he had prolonged by removing beer and fat from his diet and with therapies such as deep tissue massage. Now an abrupt union vote could bring it all to an abrupt end. It turned out he was right. He wasn't picked up by another team the following year.

I went to his ranch in Cañon City, Colorado in July of 1994 for an *SI* feature story. He was having a great time riding horses and bumping over his 50,000 acres in a jeep.

"I've never been able to be here during this time of year before," he said.

After several days photographing him at his ranch, (two "firsts" — I bunked at a player's home and that player actually asked me to stay after we finished working) we only had a pitching shot left to do. He rousted me out of bed.

"C'mon Ronnie, you gotta catch me," Gossage said, attempting to appear gruff. I was uneasy. I had no cup. No mask. The man had been clocked over 100 mph.

"C'mon. I'll go easy."

He tossed me a glove and I crouched into position. He bounced one on our pretend plate. Then he threw another one into the dirt.

This isn't so bad, I thought. "Show me what you got, Gooster!"

He threw another one. This time *hard*. It stung the palm of my hand and reverberated through my body. I tossed it back to him.

He hurled another, which hit my hand in the same spot. I grimaced and tossed it back to him.

Again, he pitched the ball to me. Hard. This one flew out of my glove. It felt like it took my thumb with it.

"Man," I said. "You almost ripped off my thumb!"

"Yeah," Gossage said. "I was careful not to mess with your trigger finger." Then he walked toward me. "Okay," he said, his mustache curling up as he grinned, "Let's go fishing."

TOMMY LASORDA
RIVERFRONT STADIUM, CINCINNATI, 1994

Doug Rader

I've been a player, coach and a manager. And your mind-set depends on where you are in your life. As a player you have no clue. You just play the game for pure joy. It's an activity that's all encompassing and fulfilling. You're wrapped up in the games and you don't think of anything but the games. As a coach, you're older and more insightful. How you deal with your manager has to do with how much respect you have for the man you're with. Notice I didn't say "working for." If you don't respect him, your relationship will be tenuous. Of course it depends on how badly you need the job.

Some coaches keep their job by being brown-nosers and keeping their mouths shut. To tell you the truth, I find it more refreshing when guys lose their temper. There's so little truth in baseball these days. As for being a manager, it's not like it used to be. To manage today, you have to be politically correct. You can't be like the old-timers, like Leo Durocher. The managers today are created entities. Their hands are tied. The days of pure honesty are gone. Organizations won't tolerate pure honesty and the press will bury you. You know the criteria by which most managers get hired today? The organizations like to say, "This guy can really handle the media." I hate that.

Bud Selig

People thought that I made the decision to cancel the World Series the year of the strike. But that's not right. I was under a lot of pressure to announce one way or another. But it was already painfully obvious the World Series was not going to be played. The players had been on strike for five weeks. You can't play the World Series without the players. So really, the decision had already been made.

When the time came, I was hoping there would be a joint announcement between the players association and myself. But the players association did not join me, which left me alone to announce it. This gave the perception that I canceled the World Series.

The whole situation led to a lot of personal attacks against me, which were incredibly painful and unfair. But that's the price you pay when you're the man in charge. You just have to move on with it.

David Justice

D espite being featured as one of *People* magazine's "50 Most Beautiful People" in 1994, David Justice was no media darling. He had a reputation for being aloof, some even said arrogant, with the media and his teammates. Then Justice married the gorgeous movie star Halle Berry in 1993, and many people said he had become an all-around nicer person, on and off the field.

In 1994, *Sports Illustrated* ran a story about the "new and improved" Justice. I had seen Justice around over the years but this was the first time I would photograph him one-on-one for a major feature. When I first approached him about the story, explaining that we needed several pictures — most importantly, one of he and Berry together — he seemed agreeable. Justice said Berry was out of town shooting the *Flintstones* movie but I could photograph him at his house the following Monday.

Monday came. I phoned his agent, Steve Wood, several times through the day and finally was told Justice was not available.

That evening, after Mark Mulvoy (*SI* managing editor at the time) told editors he wanted the story to run as soon as possible, I was instructed to offer to fly with Justice by Lear jet to the *Flintstones* set and to tell them *SI* would put them up in the hotel of their choice and return Justice to Atlanta before the next game.

"I don't want to be doing that shit on my day off," Justice said.

I then flew to Cincinnati, where the Braves were playing (also Justice's hometown), to photograph game action and get a picture of Justice with his mother, preferably at her house. For two days he put me off, then, the last day of the stand, he said his mother would be at the game that night. We could do the picture there. I waited for him after the game on the ramp leading to the locker room. When he saw me he motioned for his mother, who was wearing a sweatsuit and seemed unprepared to be photographed. He walked with her toward me and put his arm around her. I clicked off a few shots.

"That's it," he said, turning to walk up the ramp.

Back in Atlanta, I was now under deadline pressure. *SI* had already held the story for two weeks. Each day when I saw Justice at the ballpark, he would greet me saying, "Here comes the stalker," or he would simply walk away from me.

One day I went to shoot him at his house. When I arrived, Justice opened the door, said "I'm not ready," and shut the door, leaving me, Wood and my assistant standing in the heat for close to an hour, wondering whether to stay or go. When he finally returned to the door, we came in, did one picture, then Justice said that was all the time he had. We left.

Finally, through Wood, I arranged a day to shoot Justice and Berry at their home. My assistant and I met Wood at his office an hour before we were to shoot. He was stalling. It was getting closer to shoot time. "What's the deal?" I said. I had another shoot that afternoon, with Tom Glavine, and I didn't want to keep him waiting.

"Well," Wood said. "They're not quite ready. Maybe we should wait . . ."

"Let's go now," I said. "They'll be ready by the time we do all our set-up."

We went to the house. My assistant and I began setting up on the back porch while Wood went to find Justice. "They're not ready," he said. We all waited on the back porch, sweating in 95-degree heat for over an hour. Finally, Justice emerged.

"What the hell is this?" he said, looking at the lights we'd set up.

"I told you this is the most important picture," I said.

Berry came out. Justice began berating me, "I don't know what the deal is here . . . this is turning into a big deal, this is gonna take all day . . ."

My assistant busied himself adjusting lights. Wood looked down at his shoes.

I turned to Berry and said, "Halle, you're an actress and a model. You can make this picture happen in three minutes and I'm out of here. And by the way, we could have done this two weeks ago when *SI* offered to fly David to your movie set," I said.

Wood took a deep breath. Justice looked away.

"They did?" she said to Justice.

I explained my idea to her.

"I like that," she said, and led Justice by the elbow to pose next to her.

Both Berry and Justice turned it on. I got the picture I wanted immediately. It showed a loving couple bathed in gorgeous light.

Two weeks later Wood called *SI* to request prints of the shot. He then called me and left a message, "David and Halle signed a print for you. Where should I send it?" I didn't return the call.

Barry and Justice divorced in 1996.

Kirk Gibson

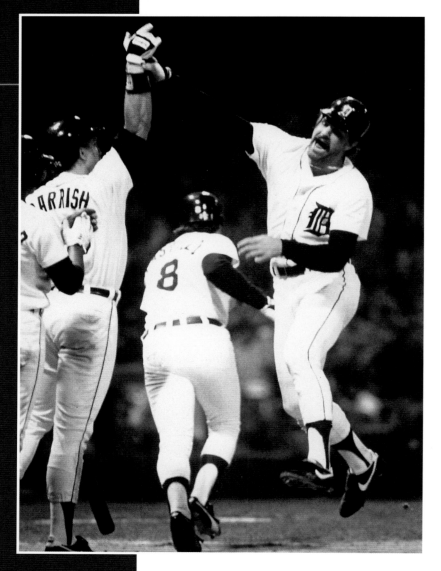

The thing I'm most proud of in baseball is that I was a World Champion. That's always been my only goal. Not to hit .300. If my team was ahead 10–0, I'd try to hit one out of the stadium and usually I struck out. I'd give an at-bat away because I didn't care about the stat sheet. Hitting .300 was important to guys like Wade Boggs. I mean, I once saw him take a perfect 3–0 pitch with runners on all the bases, just so he would get a walk. I thought, "Wow!"

As a World Champion, I tried to motivate my teammates. I was a high-energy guy. If we got our butts kicked in three games, I'd inject energy into the clubhouse to keep at bay that Beast that wants you to abandon your goals.

Of course, when I gave 100 percent and we lost, I could accept that defeat.

I've always felt that money wasn't the point of the game. All the money I made in baseball never made me happy. Being a productive member of my team made me happy. That was most important to me. I don't know what's in the minds of players always looking to renegotiate their contracts during the season. Your contract is not part of the game. That should be settled during the off-season. It shows a lack of priorities. If the game needs anything it's a return to good old basic American baseball morals.

A REFLECTION BY

Reggie Jackson

I was able to come to the ball park everyday and focus on the job I
had to do, for myself and my teammates. I learned my focus and my
drive from my father. You can't go out there and worry about what's
been written. Every thing changes from day to day.

The media attention now is even greater than in was in 1978
when I was with the Yankees. It's worse today because the media are
only looking for sensational stories now, unlike the guys I respected
like Mike Lupica and Jim Murray.

The first two years with the Yankees my relationship with
Thurman Munson was so strained over a quote attributed to me,
"I'm the straw that stirs the drink." I didn't even say that. Some
writer did. It took until 1979 for Thurman and I to finally make
amends.

In spite of all the distractions — the media, Steinbrenner, Billy
Martin — I had to always remember what my father said about
remaining focused. The problems most free agents have had coming
to New York is they get distracted by what's being said, what's being
written, instead of focusing on the job. That's playing the game.

RICK AUSTIN - WISCONSIN RAPIDS TWINS
CLINTON, IOWA, 1980

DARRELL PORTER - ST. LOUIS CARDINALS
ST. LOUIS, 1981

Greg Maddux

At the start of spring training in 1993, the big baseball story was the Braves' pitching staff, specifically the addition of former Cub and Cy Young Award winner for the previous year, Greg Maddux. Tom Glavine had been the ace of the pitching staff and now the Braves had both Maddux and Glavine, as well as John Smoltz, Steve Avery and Pete Smith in their starting rotation.

These five pitchers were thought to be unbeatable. Not a pitch had been thrown yet that season, but everybody was talking about them. Everybody wanted to photograph them together. *Sports Illustrated* was no exception.

I went to the Braves' spring training complex in West Palm Beach one morning to photograph the pitchers together for a cover. I thought I would have the starting five all to myself, but unfortunately, due to incredible demand, the Braves PR staff arranged for the pitchers to be available that day in ten-minute increments to whoever had requested time with them. I set up two situations during my time and came away with what I thought would work as a cover shot.

I needed another shot of the pitchers together on the mound for an opening picture. The PR staff left it up to me to arrange it, so two days later I returned to West Palm Beach. I went into the clubhouse, something I only do if I have specific business with a player. (I respect that this is their sanctuary.)

There were several players inside, among them Glavine, Maddux and one of the coaches, Ned Yost. I approached Maddux to tell him about the remaining picture I needed to do.

"Jesus!" he shouted, before I had finished a sentence. "What *is* this? What am I getting out of this. Am I getting any money out of this?"

"No," I said. "We don't pay for pictures."

Embarrassed and mad, I started to walk away before I said something I would regret. Tom Glavine, who was pouring himself some coffee, caught my eye and motioned me over.

"What's that all about?" I asked him.

"I don't know," Glavine said. "Just go outside and set up. I'll have everybody out there at 9:30."

Glavine, who has always been the definition of a gentleman and a man of his word, brought the other pitchers outside on cue. I did a few quick shots, but there was so much tension I could tell the picture wasn't working.

"Thanks, guys," I said.

The picture from two days earlier ran as an opener for the story, which was bumped from the cover to an inside piece.

A week or so later, I was sitting on the dugout bench before batting practice one day. Maddux came over and sat next to me.

"How'd that picture turn out?" he said.

Then we made some small talk. After about five minutes he got up and jogged over to join a coach on the field.

"Was that an apology?" my assistant asked.

"No," I said. "Being a baseball player means never having to say you're sorry."

"TODAY, YOU
NEVER KNOW YOUR
TEAMMATES FROM
YEAR TO YEAR."

WF

A REFLECTION BY

Whitey Ford

We had fun when I played with the Yankees. We didn't make much money. We all had to work winter jobs in the off-season. I worked for Mattel toys, Railway Express and on Wall Street. I didn't play the game for a living then. We were closer as teammates than guys are now because we played together for 18 years. I'm still friends with Elston Howard's wife, Rissuto, Berra, Mrs. Mantle, and all of Billy's wives (ha ha). Today, you never know your teammates from year to year. Look at the Marlins.

The big controversy with the Yankees was when we got in that fight at the Copa nightclub, but we were with our wives. Sure we fooled around a lot. Mickey and I always got in trouble. It was a lot of fun. But the most important thing about it was the money. In my first year my World Series check was bigger than my salary check. So winning the World Series became very important to us. We just wanted to support our families. I came from a blue-collar background. My father was a bartender. Today, fans resent the money players make. I don't know why. Maybe it's because of their agents and lawyers. In my day, we wouldn't dare bring an agent or a lawyer into contract negotiations.

To tell you the truth I don't like the game today. All the guys go "me, me, me." They hit a home run and stand at the plate for ten minutes to see where it goes. There are too many hot dogs.

WHITEY FORD AND MICKEY MANTLE

Michael Jordan
(The Baseball Player)

The NBA may have the Major League Baseball team owners and players' union to thank for the return of its mega star, Michael Jordan. If not for the baseball strike in 1994, Jordan may well have finished his career as a baseball player.

In 1993, Michael Jordan stunned the sports world by announcing he would quit basketball to play baseball. He showed up at the Chicago White Sox spring training facility in Sarasota, Florida and began taking batting practice and running sprints along with all the other White Sox contenders.

Jordan's spring training performance was unremarkable. The only thing extraordinary about Jordan being in camp was the crush of cameras and reporters following his every soft toss.

Sports Illustrated ran a cover story about Michael's baseball quest entitled, "Michael, Bag it!". I guess he was unhappy about the blunt commentary because when I arrived in Sarasota to shoot him at camp he told Scott Reifert, White Sox Public Relations Director, that he wouldn't come out after practice to talk to the newspaper beat writers until "the *Sports Illustrated* guys left."

So, I shot him from a distance then left so the beat guys could meet their deadlines.

Jordan played one season in Single-A ball. When he initially made the switch to baseball he had said it would take him at least two years to be ready for the big leagues. Then came the players' strike. Jordan was approached about being a replacement player, something he elected not to do. So he returned to the Chicago Bulls and resumed his phenomenal basketball career, and the world never got to see what he could have done as a baseball player.

MICHAEL JORDAN
SARASOTA, FLORIDA, 1994

Orlando Hernandez

O rlando Hernandez, known affectionately as El Duque ("the Duke"), was the star pitcher on the Cuban National Team when I photographed him in Havana in December 1995. His brother, Livan, the MVP of the 1997 World Series, had already defected and signed with the Florida Marlins when El Duque and I met.

Accompanied by an official host, I picked up El Duque at his home and suggested we find a baseball diamond. I wanted an empty place but got a delightful surprise when El Duque took me to the neighborhood ballpark where he played as a boy. The park was filled with kids. He greeted his boyhood coach with a bear hug. He then went down the line of kids sitting on a wall, all wearing different American baseball caps. He shook each boy's hand and talked to each one, slapping their backs for encouragement.

"You're a pitcher?" he asked. "Good!"

Three months after I left Cuba, the newspapers reported that El Duque was removed from the Cuban National Team due to an "injury," even though none could be confirmed by any non-Cuban journalist. He worked for a year as a physical therapist in a hospital.

Most people thought he was being punished for his brother's defection. But actually, El Duque admitted upon arriving in the United States (after escaping Cuba and arriving in the Bahamas by raft), that he had in fact been caught planning to escape.

El Duque signed a $6 million contract with the Yankees in 1998.

"HE SHOOK EACH BOY'S HAND AND TALKED TO EACH ONE, SLAPPING THEIR BACKS FOR ENCOURAGEMENT."

RCM

Ozzie Smith

As a kid I never thought much about one day being a big league baseball player. I played all sports and my mom told me to do my best. I always pursued being the best I could be, working hard and enjoying it. It wasn't until I was a junior in high school that baseball became something I wanted to do. (Maybe even in the majors!) When I first came up to the big leagues it was great to have someone like Willie Stargell for young, black players like myself to look up to. I was able to learn respect for the game from players like him. Now that I'm out of the game, and even being considered for the Hall of Fame, I know how lucky and blessed I was to play the game that I loved.

A REFLECTION BY
George Brett

In '92, I was in pursuit of my 3,000th hit. At the start of the season, I wasn't sure I was going to get there. I was 39, and I wasn't the player that I once was. I actually thought about retiring. But because of the impact that my father had on me, I just couldn't quit.

My father taught me competitiveness. He was a big boost and a big influence. He taught me that to be the best it's not only "practice makes perfect" but "perfect practice makes perfect." Even in high school, he never allowed me or my brothers to be complacent. Even if I got three hits in a game. He always pushed us to do better.

When my brother Ken and I were in the big leagues, we knew what an impact we had on Dad's life. Every morning, first thing, he'd get the newspaper. If Kansas City won and George Brett had a good day, Dad had a good day. If we lost, he would be in a miserable, kick-ass mood. I always did the best I could, because otherwise, 1,600 miles away it would ruin my Dad's day.

I lost my Dad before I got my 3,000th hit; he never saw it. But my brother Ken was the announcer for the Angels that night. After the game Ken was interviewing me in the dugout. He said, "Hopefully Dad saw this from heaven." We both had tears in our eyes.

Dad was such an important part of my life. He taught me and my brothers about the quality of life and that's what I'm trying to do with my three boys. Dad didn't live long enough to see them but I named one of my sons, Jackson, after him. I know players are supposed to be role models and I believe that. But the biggest role model in your life should always be your Dad.

"BUCK" ROGERS, 1980

B.J. SURHOFF AND JOHNNY RAY
MILWAUKEE COUNTY STADIUM, 1990

Kids in the Dominican Republic

SAN PEDRO, DOMINICAN REPUBLIC, 1995

In the winter of 1995, I went to the Dominican Republic to photograph Moises Alou and his family for a *Sports Illustrated* feature. His father, Felipe, the Montreal Expos' (and Moises') coach, also had a career as a Major League player. He and his brothers, Jesus and Mattie, all played in the Big Leagues at the same time.

I had visited the Dominican several times before and always liked it. My favorite thing about it was the baseball atmosphere; the whole country is in love with the game. Kids are seen playing everywhere. Whole towns turn out even for amateur games.

While working with the Alous, I was staying in Santo Domingo. When I had a day off, I decided to travel to San Pedro de Macoris, about a two-hour drive. I passed by this town once on a previous trip and wanted to return.

San Pedro, a poor, rural town, is famous for being the cradle of Dominican shortstops such as Tony Fernandez, Alfredo Griffin, Mariano Duncan and Jose Uribe. On my previous trip I noticed kids playing baseball everywhere. When I returned, I wasn't disappointed. Every field and yard seemed to be filled with kids engrossed in games. Even a farm field with grazing cows had a makeshift diamond.

Here was baseball in its purest form. The kids, many of whom were barefoot, didn't let a lack of equipment stop them. Bases were made of ripped-up cardboard boxes. Many kids had carved their own bats from tree limbs. The baseballs were tattered, valiantly held together with twine and tape. Most of the "teams" shared one scruffy glove between them. The kids were smiling, cheering and laughing.

It was one of my favorite days as a photographer. Because I wasn't working on an assignment, but photographing something just for myself.

"A CAREER"

Dan Quisenberry

It seems like yesterday
it seems like never
it lasted so long
it went so fast

I practiced my whole life
from daydream days
in social studies
to sandlot games
little league games
backyard games
hardball
tennis ball
whiffle ball
rock ball

early in big league years
it seemed I just had to keep the ball
in play
guys with numbers like
5 and 6 and 20
ran like retrievers
fetched the ball
brought it back
it felt like a riptide
I couldn't help going with its pull
we were good
we knew it

much gets blurred
wins, losses, races
mostly I had my head down
down in the trenches
I missed stuff
sometimes the shrapnel
but sometimes I looked up

I was lookin up when I took the ball
for the first time my rookie year
from Whitey Herzog
my knees shook
like I was getting married
Lamar Johnson drilled a two hopper
that Frank White snared with a bound
    to his right
that I never saw in minor leagues

I was lookin up when George Brett hit
    a Ruthian blast
off a guy who threw as hard as God
Willie Randolph took a called third
why didn't he swing?
it was right there
and we were series bound

I was lookin up when Janie and I had
    a girl and a boy
a fifty day strike, Marvin Miller said
"lets show 'em our muscle"
I learned to hang wallpaper
change diapers
grow tomatoes
lose golf balls

I was lookin up when it was too quiet
DEA, FBI men hovered
with our team
we looked at each other, suspicious
in the locker room
a long, hot, sweaty, losing summer

I was lookin up when it was a cool
    night in October

Darryl Motley caught
a lazy fly off Andy Van Slyke's bat
Kansas City delirious as champs
we poured champagne on sweat
    soaked heads
it burned our eyes
we didn't care
we screamed we sang we laughed
drunk with victory

I was lookin up when Dick Howser
    told us
he can't manage anymore
go on without him
more to life than baseball
he died that summer
we froze and played like statues

I was lookin up when the mirror
    showed
a red hat on my head
a different logo
it looked foreign
like in a prism
felt it too
as a defector in a new land
except Whitey again was manager

I was lookin up when I sat at a table
with reporters
telling them I quit
telling myself don't cry don't cry
    don't cry
I didn't want to break
the unwritten code of big leaguers

It lasted so long
it went so fast
it seems like yesterday
it seems like never

"A Career"
© 1998 by Dan Quisenberry.
Reprinted from *Days Like This* with the
permission of Helicon Nine Editions.